W9-BOF-216

Raising Financially Fit Kids

Raising Financially Fit Kids

REVISED

Joline Godfrey

TEN SPEED PRESS
Berkeley

Copyright © 2003, 2013 by Joline Godfrey

All rights reserved.
Published in the United States by Ten Speed Press, an imprint of the
Crown Publishing Group, a division of Random House, Inc., New York.
www.crownpublishing.com
www.tenspeed.com

Ten Speed Press and the Ten Speed Press colophon are registered trademarks
of Random House, Inc.

A previous edition of this work was published in 2003 by Ten Speed Press,
Berkeley, CA.

Library of Congress Cataloging-in-Publication Data

Godfrey, Joline.
  Raising financially fit kids / Joline Godfrey. — 2nd ed.
    p. cm.
  Includes index.
  Summary: "This combination parenting and personal finance book helps
parents teach their children key money skills—such as saving, spending,
budgeting, investing, building credit, and donating—that they'll need to
become financially secure adults"—Provided by publisher.
1. Children—Finance, Personal. 2. Teenagers—Finance, Personal.
3. Saving and investment. 4. Child rearing. I. Title.
  HG179.G626 2013
  332.0240083—dc23

Trade Paperback ISBN: 978-1-60774-408-5
eBook ISBN: 978-1-60774-409-2

Printed in China

Design by Studio Hinrichs
Production by Colleen Cain
Cover photography copyright © Jock McDonald and Hermera/Thinkstock
Interior photography copyright © Jock McDonald

10 9 8 7 6 5 4 3 2 1

Revised Edition

For Jonathan

Contents

Grace

I am blessed by people, events, and the mysteries of the cosmos. But sometimes, looking back I think, "I want a do-over. I want to re-do this period or that of my life with the knowledge I have now." But the do-over is a rare thing. Which is why I was grateful when Ten Speed Press offered the opportunity for a "do-over" of *Raising Financially Fit Kids*. I learned a great deal in the decade since the book was first published and I'm excited to share that knowledge here.

This new edition came to fruition with the support and contribution of people I've worked and learned with since the first edition was published. David Wegbreit's good mind, sensitive ear, and offbeat imagination made this book better and his contributions to the development of Stage Five will have continuing impact. And James Spears, who came to the process as David returned to graduate school, added a critical eye and judgment that sharpened the ideas I wanted to share. Both men care about excellence, and this book is better for their careful attention.

The real stories and well-tested methods described in each chapter are possible because of the collective creativity of out-of-the-box thinkers who understand that learning is a process, not an event: Ryan Harris, Sarah Frost, Karen Cahill, Sean Stein, Robin Catlin, and Ryan Liss.

My agent, Betsy Amster, has been a loyal and properly demanding advocate, making all my work better. And my editor, Lisa Westmoreland, has the gift of combining kindness and discipline to get the best from her writers. Her suggestions helped make this do-over worth doing.

And the do-over would not have been possible without Howard Milstein, the CEO of New York Private Bank and Trust. Though the descriptor of *visionary* has become clichéd, it is a worthy and authentic title for a man who is a builder—of businesses and buildings, big ideas and grand possibilities. Howard understands that work that lasts takes time—he is the entrepreneurs' entrepreneur, and his support of this particular entrepreneur gave us legs to last and learn. If the ideas in this book have impact, it is because Howard gave us time and resources to bring them to life.

And by no means least, I am graced by the teaching I receive from the children and families I work with, unnamed here to respect their privacy. The most effective education is dynamic, engaged, reciprocal. It is learning in the context of human connection. There is nothing more exciting than working with intentional families and curious kids—lessons learned with them are woven throughout this book.

Foreword

Toward the end of 2007, the U.S. financial market began its largest decline in seventy-five years. As the markets plummeted, millions of Americans watched in shock as the values of their assets, retirement plans, and homes plunged. Four years later, in the aftermath of the financial crisis of 2008, the financial world rests upon delicate footing. Unemployment remains stubbornly high. The financial industry is in the midst of significant reform. Most people's home values and personal wealth levels have yet to recover fully. Yet the pace of change in the financial marketplace seems to be speeding up, not slowing.

Over the last twenty years, the financial industry has created a dizzying array of financial products and financial options. Whether one is attempting to mortgage her home, establish a retirement account, simply open a bank account, or gain some exposure to the U.S. stock market, it has never been more challenging to navigate the complex financial marketplace around us and to feel confident with the various financial decisions one must make. If that alone is not enough to digest, today the U.S. Tax Code (more specifically, Title 26 of the U.S. Code of Federal Regulations—the portion written by the IRS) is 16,845 pages long.

Similarly, the instant access to information that the Internet has enabled is both a blessing and a curse; while it may be easier to get answers to most of one's financial questions at the push of a few buttons, there also is far more information than ever before to sift through and digest.

In this daunting world of financial complexity, Joline Godfrey has come to the rescue. In her book *Raising Financially Fit Kids* Joline provides parents of kids of all ages with a series of relevant, easy-to-grasp financial tools to assist them in raising children with a healthy set of financial values and a degree of financial fluency. These are among the tools that *all* adolescents need in order to navigate successfully through an increasingly complex financial world.

As the Chinese philosopher Laozi encouragingly offered, "a journey of a thousand miles begins with a single step." In similar fashion, one's financial education can be—and I would argue *should* become—a lifelong pursuit of self-discovery and self-improvement. While many experts in the field recommend that parents begin their children's financial education when they become teenagers, Joline astutely challenges this view. She encourages parents to start their children's financial literacy at the age of five.

As my grandfather Irving Harris, a pioneer in the early childhood development field, often reminded me, learning begins at birth, and it continues for as long as one is open-minded to the integration of new ideas. Children who start to practice the basic concepts of counting, saving, and spending at a younger age have more time to practice and master these skills. In his book *Outliers: The Story of Success*, Malcolm Gladwell asserts the extremely high correlation between preparation and success. Essentially, the earlier in life one begins, the more one can practice. The more one practices, the more competent one is likely to become. Financial education is no exception. In this manner, Joline's book provides parents with a wonderful set of tools to enable them to begin their own children's financial education as soon as they are ready to start learning and which will continue to provide families with age-appropriate financial education guidance as adolescents begin to spread their wings.

Whereas many books of this type simply provide parents with a basic set of formulaic suggestions and exercises, *Raising Financially Fit Kids* elegantly connects the dots between parenting and financial education, and the fundamental interconnectedness of these with children's physical, intellectual, social, and emotional development. As a pioneer in the financial education field with deep roots in clinical social work, education, and early childhood development, Joline has successfully developed a program that is simultaneously nuanced and straightforward to follow. In other words, parents who are secretly unsure of their own ability to provide their children with appropriate guidance needn't worry; this book is certain to provide comfort even to the most apprehensive parents.

In recognition of the fact that children's intellectual and emotional capabilities develop over time, Joline has divided her book into several sections, each of which is developmentally appropriate to a specific age range. Along the way, she explains the complex relationships between a child's saving, spending, and earning habits and his or her self-esteem, and the ways in which children's developing relationship with money can be influenced by the establishment and reinforcement of a solid set of financial values and habits. She also provides parents with a broad array of tools that are easy to utilize and which will help to destigmatize a subject that too often seems taboo.

After all, money itself is neither intrinsically benign nor evil. Rather, it simply is a tool—which, if utilized responsibly, can enable people to become and stay independent, achieve their financial (and/or philanthropic) goals, and generally lead more productive and fulfilling lives.

While the financial world may seem endlessly complex and at times awfully intimidating, this book is just the opposite. Parents who doubt their own financial competence should relax, for help is on the way! Whether your own family is of sizable wealth or modest means, *Raising Financially Fit Kids* will provide *all* parents with a set of easy-to-understand tools to assist them in raising children to become savvy, self-confident, financially independent adults who have mastered a solid set of social and financial skills and values.

As Joline poses in her book, "What kind of child do you want to raise?"
I hope that you will turn the page and find out.

Jack Polsky, CEO
William Harris Investors, Inc.

Preface to the Second Edition

Two events made this new edition of *Raising Financially Fit Kids* worth doing. The first was a meeting in Racine, Wisconsin, in 2006. The stock market was ascendant, real estate prices were over the moon, and every middle class family looked at the new "value" of that little ranch they'd been living in for twenty years and suddenly felt the thrill of being a newly minted millionaire. The 99 percent all thought they had suddenly entered the hallowed halls of the 1 percent—though at that time we did not have these terms for the country's economic disparity. The new "home equity loan"—a brilliant and absurdly easy way to tap one's new "millionaire" status—meant that every kid could have all the new games and toys emerging from Silicon Valley, as well as a car when he or she turned sixteen, a fresh logo-inscribed wardrobe every season, and $300 sneakers if that's what it took to make them happy.

Paris Hilton's antics, dogs, purses, friends, TV shows, and pronouncements ("Every woman should have four pets in her life: a mink in her closet, a jaguar in her garage, a tiger in her bed, and a jackass who pays for everything") had the effect of unhinging parents everywhere (except her own, apparently). A new language was emerging. "Affluenza" was a code word describing the affliction of children whose parents gave them every material good that money could buy in the name of love. Any parents with a TV were suddenly scared to death that *their* kids would grow up to be shallow, conspicuous consumers with no real purpose in life. (In fairness, it must be noted that young Paris grew up to be quite the entrepreneur and may have been a more interesting character than she was given credit for at the time—but I digress.)

In those days, two realities became more pronounced: on the one hand, amped-up consumerism, driven by easy access to credit and wealth; and on the other hand, a growing anxiety felt by parents who were uneasy about the impact of a culture in which reality shows celebrated materialism and national heroes were known more for their bling than for their character.

"How," parents wanted to know, "in a culture of consumption and wealth, can we raise kids to be financially thoughtful, frugal, generous, and savvy?"

Those were genuinely complicated days to be parenting. In response, twelve families decided to hold a meeting in Racine, Wisconsin, to explore and answer the question: what should families do to prepare their children for the responsibilities of money management? What set those twelve families meeting in Racine apart is that they came together, of their own volition, to tackle an aspect of parenting that, up to that point, had been mostly ignored. The collective consciousness of the time seemed to be that kids would somehow, on their own, figure out how to function as economic beings. *Of course* they'd learn to budget, earn income, allocate income and earnings appropriately, and save.

This was, of course, a fantasy. Children who had cell phones at twelve (and younger), cars at sixteen, and "the bank of Dad," as writer David Owen aptly named it, would not easily acquire financial skills and financial responsibility. The Racine group's acknowledgment of this was a watershed moment. Over the course of the weekend, it emerged that the group wanted to build a framework for raising financially fluent children—and as I left Racine at the end of the workshop, I understood that this work represented a sea change. Over time, financial education would become as normal and routine for these families as piano lessons, SAT coaching, and college tours.

And since 2006, that is exactly what happened. Intentional thought-leader families have used this book (and others), as well as the curriculum that emerged from the first edition of this book (The Great Families Program), to raise financially fit kids. These forward-thinking families, like their early-adopter counterparts in the high-tech world, found themselves on the cutting edge—the first to try out ideas that may have at first seemed strange and unnecessary.

I am grateful for those families—we've taught each other a great deal as we've created, tested, and revised methods and materials to help kids acquire financial fluency. But there were long nights when I worried that the ideas shared in the first edition of this book would never gain true currency; that the programs and services I'd spent years to design and make effective and fun would never grow large enough to make my company viable.

And then . . . the second event presented itself.

It was September 26, 2008, a bleak, drizzly Saturday morning. The people streaming into Morgan Hall at the Harvard Business School (HBS) had endured a battering week. Stock markets were plummeting, and many in the group had suffered significant financial losses. The story unfolding during those autumn weeks and afterward would leave few in that audience—indeed, few across the entire country—unscathed.

But while everyone else was fixated on the enormous black cloud gathering overhead, I was already looking for the silver lining. There is nothing like a crisis to open ears, hearts, and minds, and this crisis was a doozy. "At last," I thought, "a teachable moment!"

By 2008 I had been giving talks to HBS alumni groups for a number of years.[1] I always enjoyed big, engaged, attentive audiences. Smart, high-achieving parents are eager and open to tools that help them navigate the river of parenthood.

But I knew this day was going to be different—if only because the anxiety level of the audience was unprecedented. The expectancy in the air was palpable. Both inexperienced and seasoned parents wanted to know: how do we talk with our kids about what is unfolding? And how do we give them tools to be more financially secure than we feel today?

I opened by asking them: "How many of you have spoken with your children about what is going on in the stock market?"

With over three hundred people in the room, only three raised their hands. One dad reported he'd taken the occasion to explain "sub-prime" to his nine-year-old daughter; another said he'd been on the phone with his son, who'd called to ask whether they needed to cancel vacation plans. "But," he added, "I haven't talked with my son for such a long time in years. The upside is that the news is giving us an opportunity to talk!" A third parent said his daughter wanted to know whether they were now "poor."

---

1. Before you Google me: no, I do not have an MBA from HBS; I have a master's in social work from Boston University. There was, in those days, a policy dictating that only HBS grads could talk to HBS alumni. But Howard Stevenson, Sarofim-Rock Professor Emeritus of the HBS, had heard me speak, read my other book at the time, agreed to write the foreword for the first edition of this book, and felt that HBS parents and grandparents could use the information I had to share on *Raising Financially Fit Kids*. Howard is a force of nature—and I'm grateful he felt strongly enough about the topic to make what I imagine was a fairly autocratic decision at the time. To him, my deepest gratitude.

Of course, what this told the other 297 parents and grandparents present was that there was no magic message to share about the national angst being reported on TV, in the paper, and in family kitchens across the nation. The important thing was to *talk*—to share reality with kids as much as possible, so they do not either exaggerate their fears about a family crisis (and thus stress needlessly) or turn a blind eye, losing the capacity to adapt and contribute to meeting the normal challenges of being a family.

What Is Different in This Edition?

Do-overs in life are rare and magical. So when asked to update and revise *Raising Financially Fit Kids*, I reflected on these two events. As a result, this new edition is different in four ways.

1. Everything is updated. David Wegbreit, who worked with me on this new edition, pointed out (gently, to his credit) that there are technologies mentioned routinely in the first edition that no longer exist. I suspect there is no getting around the fact that the world our children interact with routinely is, for many of us, the stuff of Ray Bradbury short stories. Throughout the book, I've updated cultural and technological touchstones and added new resources.

2. We deal with twenty-somethings. The first book ended with Stage Four, financial education for kids up to the age of eighteen. Young adults were an afterthought, and I assumed they would use other resources to become financially fluent. The problem is, there are few "other resources" that effectively teach financial skills for the twenty-first century. As the recession and high unemployment levels altered the future for even the most well-educated and best-connected of young adults, we realized that not dealing with twenty-somethings was like abandoning eighteen-year-old kids who age out of foster care: it was premature and ethically wrong. To set this right, this edition includes Stage Five, a new chapter dedicated to twenty-somethings.

3. The basic skills are different, but not too different. Over the last decade, the Ten Basic Money Skills I introduced in the first edition of the book (see page 2) have proven to be a great framework for showing parents what kids absolutely need to know to be financially fit. But, as I've learned, they weren't perfect. Two of the skills seemed redundant, but more important, we had

ignored a skill that over the last decade has become increasingly necessary: understanding what's going on outside any one country's borders. Isolationism will not be an option for the next generation. They are already more globally connected than the wildest sci-fi imaginings could have predicted. As we have seen, economic tremors that begin halfway around the world are soon felt at home (and vice versa). Given this, we've combined the original Money Skill 2 (How to keep track of money) with Money Skill 6 (How to live within a budget) and added a new Money Skill 10: How to be a citizen of the world.

4. We're all different. The first edition was written ten years ago. I came to this work with a deep well of experience, good stories, and involvement with families that take learning and developing family strengths seriously. But we were just getting started. Nine years later, I feel like my grandmother's concert piano—all the keys have been played with a range and subtlety not available to a beginner. And the families we work with represent a wealth of differences: multiple generations dispersed around the world, blended families with children of multiple races and nationalities, single parents, and same-sex parenting pairs.

This diversity has resulted in work that both begins earlier (we see lots of families who begin mindfully with children at three and four) and continues as lifelong learning. Parents no longer dismissively say of their adult children, "It's too late." Now they give them resources for becoming fiscally fit as routinely as they send them off to language immersion classes and fitness trainers. Which is simply to say that I think this book is better because (1) we're better and have more to offer, and (2) the families that come to it are more thoughtful and intentional than ever before.

What's Not Different?
Core ideas endure.

A big one is that this book is not just about the money. If anything, this became more clear in the course of the last ten years, and the original emphasis we put on developing human capital in tandem with financial capital has been amplified. Like the first edition, this book aims to help you launch great kids: independent, balanced, and able to exercise good judgment, practice responsible habits, and live independent lives as contributing members of both family and community. Throughout the book you will encounter examples of best practices we have observed from the families we work with.

You will see more references to the development of "human capital"—the unique skills, knowledge, talents, and values that make each of us unique and combine to make each family strong. What does it matter how much money kids earn, inherit, or create if they do not also have the values to manage that money with integrity and mindfulness? And what does it matter how hard families work to give their kids a sound financial safety net if those children cannot sustain—and mend holes in—that net when needed? Finally, what is the importance of any level of wealth if young people do not develop values and vision to use financial capital for something of great purpose and meaning?

My life's work has been with children. I can say with total clarity—having encountered thousands of children in my career and logged considerably more than the ten thousand hours Malcolm Gladwell suggests are necessary to claim expertise—that the children who become most at peace as adults are those who *know who they are.* These adults are never just their bank accounts, their cars, or their logos. Even the most obsessed car collectors or the most stylish fashionistas are deeper than the composite materials in their cars and fabrics. If they are at peace (at least sometimes—we *are* talking about humans here), it is because they have a set of values that function as a moral compass, an internal sounding bell for what's really important in their lives.

The children who become most content as adults learn to use their resources in ways that give them deep satisfaction. Some find careers that allow them to continue growing and learning; others build companies that reflect some interest, knowledge, or passion; and others find ways to be of service—in NGOs, military, government, nonprofits, and public and social service.

These adults understand that money, well managed, allows them the luxury of living lives of meaning—whether that means balancing the budget of the school they manage, finding ways to grow the food bank they run, or investing in companies that provide a critical (or just a fun) product or service. Young people who learn to manage both their human and financial capital are more at peace—and effective—than those kids who have learned to manage only one or the other. So in this edition, we take pains to emphasize this dual approach to financial education—repeatedly.

The second enduring truth is that this book is not about income level. Whether your family has vast resources that allow for significant trust funds for kids or you are on a fixed income and struggle to make ends meet, the issues parents confront with children are often fundamentally similar. Teaching children to make ends meet and shepherd wealth are the concerns of *all* parents—and parental frustration over children who haven't mastered the habits of conservative spending and liberal saving cuts across race, class, culture, and political orientation.

This book is not about raising young tycoons, Nobel laureates in economics, or fledgling investment bankers. Nor is it about pushing kids toward a premature consciousness of material wealth. Rather, it is a means for helping families prepare the next generation to thrive in a global economy. It's a tool for teaching kids to attain independence and sustain financial safety nets. And it's an aid to help families walk the line between overprotecting kids from the real aspects of finance as a life skill and forcing them into an anxious preoccupation with money as a source of power and well-being.

Introduction: Financial Literacy Is Economic Self-Defense

Boom-and-bust markets, war and peace, health and illness, and marriage and divorce are just a few of the highs and lows that affect every life. Wise parents know that financially self-sufficient kids are less vulnerable to the vicissitudes of life. All parents' deepest desire is that their children will never need to worry about where the next meal will come from or take jobs they hate "just for the money." And that instinct—protecting kids from the harsh realities of the economics of life—sometimes gets in the way of giving them financial education, a basic tool for economic self-defense.

This book introduces the Ten Basic Money Skills that collectively provide a primer of financial knowledge. These skills offer a protective armor, preparing kids for life's challenges without scaring them to death. The activities in the book teach the Ten Basic Money Skills incrementally, defusing the tensions that seem to be ever present in the realm of kids and money.

The Ten Basic Money Skills

1. How to save

2. How to get paid what you are worth

3. How to spend wisely

4. How to talk about money

5. How to live within a budget

6. How to invest

7. How to exercise the entrepreneurial spirit

8. How to handle credit

9. How to use money to change the world

10. How to be a citizen of the world

Money and the Developmental Stages

Money struggles between parents and their kids are not an indication of failed parenting skills or financial ineptitude. While twentieth-century psychologists were deconstructing the developmental tasks of childhood as they related to motor skills, communications, and relationship capacity, they neglected to consider economic development as one of the basic developmental tasks of the child. That was a mistake, for personal economic growth is a lifelong process that has distinct stages not unrelated to the other developmental tasks of childhood. The following chart illustrates stages we all pass through in the course of our lives.

Few adults reading this book had a formal financial apprenticeship. If you were lucky, you had a parent or grandparent who offered sound guidance, but more than likely you were on your own—and that was mostly okay. Pre-1980s, our financial lives were much less complex: more aspects of banking were regulated, more companies offered pensions, and although you could add to savings accounts and develop hard assets like real estate, it wasn't possible to buy stock or create IRAs on your own. Individuals had limited access to financial transactions until the Internet and deregulation converged to give us all "greater opportunity."

Key Stages of Financial Development

Stages	Responsibilities	Actions
Apprenticeship (5–18)	Develop financial vocabulary; establish early financial habits and values; practice saving, spending, earning, and philanthropy.	Manage allowance; hold first job; begin community involvement.
Starting Out (19–30)	Establish identity and core values, independent lifestyle, experimentation, and discovery.	Acquire education, competencies, life/career experiences; establish savings and a good credit record.
Taking Charge (31–50)	Build assets; establish a foundation for self and/or family.	Acquire assets; build career and family; lead; explore life interests.
Looking Ahead (51–65)	Take stock; mentor; reinvent; contribute to next-generation needs.	Reassess life choices and goals; reenergize plans.
Reflection/Redefinition (66+)	Rethink priorities and responsibilities; plan for the next generation.	Live and give creatively.

Which helps explain why, although 75 percent of parents think that providing financial guidance for their kids is a moral imperative, only 36 percent report having any clarity on how to do that. Up until the last thirty years, the very idea of financial education was relegated to economics classes (which do little to inform kids about personal finance) and MBA programs, which do even less to teach kids about personal finance (with all due respect).

Today, post–Bernie Madoff, post the subprime meltdown, post the democratization of the financial system, and even as the Occupy Movement soldiers on, we know that good financial habits are not acquired through osmosis. They are acquired like a good backhand in tennis or a complicated dance step, through instruction, coaching, and practice, practice, practice.

Grown-ups who catch themselves thinking, "I missed my own financial apprenticeship," will find the stages and activities charts are so hands-on and experiential that, like Captain Kirk in a *Star Trek* time warp, you'll get a chance to enjoy an apprenticeship of your own while guiding the next generation.

The Financial Apprenticeship Years

Recognition of the financial apprenticeship underscores the time it takes to master skills that serve a lifetime. One can no more master financial skills in a day than one can earn a spot at Carnegie Hall in a week or speak Mandarin in a month. The process takes time—and practice.

This book takes readers through each of the apprenticeship stages, providing relevant experiences with tangible, immediate payback connected to each specific age and stage.

The Life/Money Map on pages 6–7 offers a condensed visual explanation of social/emotional experiences that are unfolding in tandem with the acquisition of financial skills. The chart is the "skeleton" followed throughout the book as we lay out tasks and activities to engage kids in the process of becoming financially fluent.

How the Book Works

In Part One, Getting Started, I explore the dramas and challenges of raising financially thoughtful kids in a culture that undermines parents' best instincts.

Part Two, The Financial Apprenticeship, gets down to business: this is the core of the book and the place you'll find activities and suggestions for making the apprenticeship as much fun for your kids as a day at Disneyland (well, almost). Building on the Ten Basic Money Skills, each chapter addresses a separate stage of the apprenticeship years: 5–8; 9–12; 13–15; 16–18, and (the formerly underserved state of young adulthood) 19–30.

Let's assume for a minute you've come across this book when your child is fourteen rather than six, and you're sure that he is clueless about money. Should you despair? No. Remember, this is a *developmental*, not a chronological, approach to raising financially fit kids. If your child is chronologically a teen but developmentally a Stage One apprentice with skills more akin to a seven- or eight-year-old's, go back and use those activities and resources as your starting place. You'll need to modify them slightly—you aren't going to ask your seventeen-year-old to spell "save" with pudding—but they should give you an idea of what you need to teach. You'll find that teens—and young adults—can cover ground pretty quickly.

It's also possible that your ten-year-old will be ready for the challenges of activities listed in the section for teens. Don't be afraid to follow your child's instincts. If you've been active about the apprenticeship early on, kids will be eager to speed up the process. Go for it. The Life/Money Map's "age/stage" designations are intended as guides for working with children through time, not as a track you can't get off of.

Part Three, Side Trips, covers Raising Young Philanthropists, It's Not Just About the Kids, and Frequently Asked Questions, which offers a quick overview of most common kids-and-money challenges. In case of emergency, turn there first.

Throughout the book, I present a host of ideas, techniques, and activities to try with your kids. Don't feel you need to cover them all. Just choose those that are most applicable to your family—and the most fun.

If you're looking for more, you'll be able to extend your experience or take it in smaller servings online. Subscribe or follow us on our various social media platforms:

Twitter: @RFFKBook
Facebook.com/RaisingFinanciallyFitKids
www.RFFK.com
rffk@independentmeans.com

The Life/Money Map

Age/Stage	Social/Emotional Development	Money Skills to Master	Challenges	Activities
Stage One: 5–8	Is curious Has short attention span May have high energy Begins to view fairness as important	Counts coins and bills Understands the value and purpose of money Learns to differentiate between wants and needs Begins to develop an ethical compass	Distinguishing between magic and reality	Acquire language. Practice financial habits.
Stage Two: 9–12	Is growing fast, body changing Feels self-conscious Begins to exhibit self-expression and independence Begins to develop social conscience Becomes aware of hobbies and careers Identifies with peer groups	Can make change Shows initiating behavior and entrepreneurial spirit Shows awareness of costs and earned money Can balance a simple checking account and keep up with a savings account	Being taken seriously; taking responsibility	Gain basic skills. Make choices based on inner values.
Stage Three: 13–15	Focuses on the present; has only a vague sense of the future Is egocentric, self-conscious, and anxious about personal behavior Begins to think independently Conforms to peer group norms and behaviors Tries on different roles in a highly experimental phase	Learns to shop comparatively Comprehends relationship of time to money Begins to earn money; initiates small ventures Commits to saving goals Develops basic understanding of investment Connects money and future Understands philanthropy Decodes bank statements Understands interest and dividends	Exercising moral choices	Practice independent action and financial decisions.

The Life/Money Map

Age/ Stage	Social/Emotional Development	Money Skills to Master	Challenges	Activities
Stage Four: 16–18	Has increased capacity for logical thought and planning Is preoccupied with acceptance by peer group Experiments with independence Confronts serious life and moral decisions	Actively saves, spends, invests Connects goals and saving Experiences responsibility for self and others Is able to talk about money and plan future Understands money as power Can read a paycheck, do simple tax forms Shows developing capacity for economic self-sufficiency	Handling conflicting desires for support and independence	Think about long-term financial goals. Develop and manage a budget.
Stage Five: 19+	Balances freedom with new responsibilities (apartment lease, first home, medical care, independent living, and so on) Finds long-term companions and love Begins to develop a strong sense of self and mastery in career or other endeavors Develops a social or moral conscience and/or a sense of faith or religious conviction	Manages cash flow Designs and manages an annual financial plan Commits and executes on saving and investing goals; understands and contributes to a diverse investment portfolio Is cognizant of the responsibilities and obligations of paying taxes Applies money, time, or talent to philanthropic contribution Engages in financial conversations with a consideration of core values and productive outcomes Knows how to make a job, not just take a job Understands why and how to develop strong credit ratings	Managing access to capital and independence	Establish a saving and credit record. Acquire an education and life/ career experience. Gain independence and demonstrate self-sufficiency.

Getting Started

"We carry our homes within us, which enables us to fly."

JOHN CAGE

From Safety Nets to Self-Sufficiency

Families function as a child's safety net, but as we saw in the 2008 meltdown, it's hard, even in the family, to *guarantee* safety. What parents and mentors *can* do is help children acquire the Ten Basic Money Skills, giving them skills to knit their own nets and acquire the capacity for self-reliance as they grow older. As Federal Reserve Chairman Ben Bernanke put it in a 2008 news conference, "In light of the problems that have arisen in the subprime mortgage market, we are reminded of how critically important it is for individuals to become financially literate at an early age so that they are better prepared to make decisions and navigate an increasingly complex financial marketplace."

A Stone in the Pond

Acting on just a few of the practices suggested in this book will be like tossing a small stone into a pond: ripples will spread out in waves you cannot measure. So relax, have fun, and remember, anything you do will put you in an advanced parenting class, as doing something is better than doing nothing—which is what many families revert to when it comes to financial education.

But to start, let's take stock of three things:

1. **Money styles.** What are the dominant behaviors each child exhibits? This information will help direct each child's financial learning plan.
2. **Your human capital inventory.** You can probably detail your financial capital—real estate, savings accounts, investments, anything that contributes to your financial net worth. But can you list your human capital? This information will give the whole family a better understanding of how and why the financial apprenticeship is worth the time and trouble involved.
3. **Your readiness.** I have yet to meet a family that doesn't have good intentions to raise a financially fit child. Every parent wants to help their kids acquire skills and knowledge to become financially safe and successful— whatever that means in the context of your family. But the families that succeed have more than vague "good intentions." They have *intention*. And they act on that intention. Coming to grips with your own readiness for the process will tell you whether to keep reading or put this book aside until you are ready—because it's a commitment.

So if you're ready, let's begin!

Money Styles

What works for raising one child may be useless for another. "My kids are completely different," I often hear. "One spends everything as soon as he gets it. The other won't let go of a penny." Sound familiar?

The hoarder is the child with a secret stash of cash. She may have no purpose  for this other than enjoying the knowledge that the money is there and watching the pile grow. These kids are unimpressed by compound interest because it is such an abstract concept and less satisfying than actually feeling the fibers of the bills stacked neatly in their hiding spot. The hoarder is a child who, when you suggest she contribute some of her savings to the cost of the new toy she wants, will give up the toy rather than cut into her hoard. Is this a problem? For the most part, kids who save in such a disciplined manner are to be rewarded (lots of parents long to see this quality in their kids). However, hoarding behavior can augur a focus on money for its own sake and can hamper good management habits down the road.

One teen told me about losing $200 she'd saved in her small change purse when she was seven years old. "I just liked seeing and counting it," she recalled. This pleasure was interrupted one Sunday when, on taking the small purse to church, she somehow dropped it and never saw it again. Even so, it took her many years to be convinced that a bank was a better bet than her change purse!

The Spendthrift

The spendthrift gets a gift of money from Aunt Jane and can't wait to spend it. Or waits for that first income tax return with plans to spend every dollar (and then some), because it's "found" money. For these kids, money equals a lack of impulse control. Although the carpe diem nature of these kids is to be

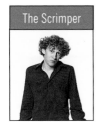
The Scrimper

applauded, if allowed to run amok, it portends trouble down the road. And if the spendthrift is the child of affluence, that brings its own set of complications.

The scrimper watches every penny and takes pleasure in saving, choosing less over more every time. Different from the hoarder, this child spends money but always chooses the less expensive option and finds great satisfaction in coming home with money left over. Though scrimpers are great savers and should be encouraged, as with all these styles, the hazard lies in the extremes. These are the kids who may grow up to be "penny wise and pound foolish" if they do not understand how to make critical financial decisions—and they may have trouble being generous with others. In business, the scrimper may be a start-up genius but may also fall prey to chronically underresourcing projects and employees, worrying about scarcity until it is a self-fulfilling prophecy that becomes reality.

The Giver

The giver is the first to organize a car wash for charity. She lends friends money when they go shopping or out for a meal. And he is always the one to pay for drinks when he and his buddies go out for the night. For the giver, generosity is no problem, but it may mask discomfort with conflict and a tendency to use money to smooth over awkward or potential conflicting situations. Givers sometimes have a hard time saving, as they can always see the yawning needs of others or may simply have a hard time saying no to the demands of others. Mentoring the giver means providing strategies for setting boundaries while encouraging generosity at the same time. For young kids this can be a complex lesson; for older children it may be hard to practice and will require lots of support from role models.

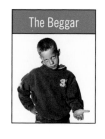
The Beggar

The beggar has insatiable needs and thrusts a hand out for something at every turn. Although this behavior may be the result of unintentional training on the part of parents (always bringing home a gift for the least reason, reinforcing a steady state of expectation), it may also be a sign of other needs, unfilled in more vital ways (attention, time, nurturing). As the beggar grows older, he may become the entitled child who will be shunned when the "cute" tactics of childhood have become less attractive.

The hustler sees a "deal" in every transaction. An allowance may be just a

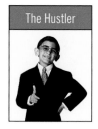
The Hustler

starting point for the kid who will try to double, triple, and leverage financial gifts or income in as many ways as possible. With all the signs of an accomplished negotiator, this child may be financially precocious, offering parents multiple opportunities for early coaching. But this may also be the child who needs help developing a moral compass to balance her transactional approach to money.

The oblivious child simply refuses to focus on money. "Whatever" may be his most common response to your attempts to engage him in any sort of conversation related to money and responsibility. Intuiting that attention to this matter opens a Pandora's box of accountability, the oblivi-

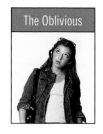
The Oblivious

ous child may reject the idea of an allowance. This is the child who, if not required to become intentional about money, will chronically abdicate responsibility to others. (There is some correlation between this style and the investors who signed on with Bernie Madoff: "I don't want to have to think about my investments.")

With all due respect to Drs. Freud, Jung, and the like, there is no solid evidence that any of these traits can be blamed on Mom, Dad, DNA, or the excesses of the baby boom generation. Particularly when a hoarder, a hustler, and a giver live in the same family, it's hard to figure out how kids pick up their money styles. Happily, whether you're dealing with a six-year-old or a sixteen-year-old, a spendthrift or a compulsive saver, there are ways to engage each of them in his or her own financial education—but it requires the use of different tactics for different kids. Financial education is not a "one size fits all" practice. It's a "whatever works" process. And the allowance is a parent's best friend when it comes to developing strategies that will work for each child.

In Part Two you can choose from activities that will encourage financial consciousness and fitness. Some work better with oblivious kids, others are perfect for the young hustler. And as parents and kids become more self aware about the advantages and drawbacks of the various styles—you can use the styles to help kids become more financially competent.

Human Capital

Some kids develop profligate habits even with parents who are themselves the soul of responsible money management. But you will always have greater standing to make demands and set expectations about financial behavior if your values about money are explicit in the family and if you are walking the talk. The True Wealth Audit is my invention, inspired by the work of Jay Hughes, author of *Family Wealth: Keeping It in the Family*. We use it to help families talk about what's really important in the family—and to give context to *why* financial education is as important as learning to read and tie your shoelaces. The activity below helps you create a True Wealth Audit of your own. To get started, we examine the four basic forms of True Wealth that every family can claim:

1. Human capital could be your grandmother's handmade quilt that she carried across the country as a young wife or the story of your grandfather's origins. It may be the work ethic you share with your sister or the love of hiking and the camping trips that are a tradition among cousins. It may be your daughter's voice and your son's love of animals. It's anything that makes your family its own weird, wonderful, unique, never-before and never-again self. It's legacy, passion, family history, and values. Our human capital allows us each to say *This is who I am*. You can have the world's largest bank

account, but if you do not have a memory or an awareness of what's deeply important in your family, the financial capital represented in that bank account will have little meaning.

2. **Intellectual capital** is the experience your brother developed when he built a house; it's the cake recipe your aunt inherited from her great-great grandmother. It's your twelve-year-old's ability to program a new app and your teen's mastery of Mandarin. It's the academic degrees you've earned and the life knowledge you've acquired. I list my ability to build a fire in the Maine woods and bake a memorable blueberry pie as part of my intellectual capital. Intellectual capital is what you know and have learned that can be used and leveraged to enhance your family. Children all across the economic spectrum who are made aware of their human and intellectual capital are reassured to see that money is not what defines them. What defines each of us is who we are: what expertise we have acquired, what makes us unique.

3. **Social capital** is not just the number of friends you have on Facebook. It's your membership on boards. It's the good will you've built in the community. It's the relationships you have built while helping out at a food bank or working on a political campaign. It's participation in your synagogue or church or charitable group and the parent group at your children's school. It's the networks you contribute to that you can also turn to for support.

4. **Financial capital** in this context refers to financial fluency, not the balance in your bank account. It's the ability to read an income statement, assess a business plan, read the business pages of the newspaper, manage a basic budget, keep a FICO score above 750, and so on. Financial capital is financial intelligence and resources.

Now, to create your True Wealth inventory, gather the family (kids six and over are fully capable of understanding and contributing to this) and list everything you can collectively think of to inventory. Keep this listing of your different types of capital and review and update it regularly. You can use this form to make your inventory.

Assets	Strengths	Concerns	Actions
Human Capital Values, beliefs Individual and family passions Gender and generational differences Heritage and legacy Awareness and psychological sophistication Storytelling and mentoring capacity			
Intellectual Capital Education, knowledge Expertise Communication skills Leadership capacity Advisors, trustees			
Social Capital Social networks Philanthropic philosophy, action Family foundation Social investments Community involvement			
Financial Capital Financial roles and responsibilities Professional advisors Portfolio literacy Legal structures Wealth transfer process Estate plans Beneficiary and trustee roles Family banking relationships			

What does your inventory tell you? What is important in your family? What relationships, knowledge, and values do you have as a group that you can claim as the foundation of your family?

The True Wealth Audit gives families a language for talking about values. It helps prioritize what's important and makes plain what you want to be intentional about. Families with *good intentions* think about family traditions, occasionally remember a wonderful family story, and are grateful for the skills and talents in the family. Families with *intention* use this inventory to focus on what's important and make plans to nurture and develop their True Wealth—the same way they nurture and develop their financial capital. It's all connected.

It's unlikely that members of any family will ever be in lockstep when it comes to their values. And it's important to acknowledge such disparities in a way that makes you a credible money mentor to your own kids. Whether you think of yourself as conservative or liberal, religious or agnostic (or just skeptical in all sorts of ways) is of less significance than that you understand the impact your beliefs have on the values—and the behaviors related to money—that emerge in your family. The True Wealth inventory is just one way to make explicit what your family's values are.

Readiness of Kids

In many homes the harangue is the same:

"Do you think I'm made of money?"

"Money doesn't grow on trees."

"Can't you do anything but spend, spend, spend?"

"If you can't save, I'll take away your allowance."

No doubt you can add some old favorites of your own to this list. Teaching kids about money is often an exercise in giving commands, making rules, and giving little (and sometimes endless) lectures. In a few homes this actually works. But in the age of action sports, motion-sensing games, and social media, experience rules. And your big competitors (iPads and smartphones, Facebook and Twitter, reality TV and 3D movies, among others) know that. For most kids—indeed, adults too—experiential, interactive learning is more fun, more engaging, and more effective than a sermon. This is borne out by the responses of kids who, when asked about the most helpful things their parents have done, respond with a story about some very practical action on the part of the parents.

Brooke, for example, tells this story:

When I was twelve, my parents sat me down one night and explained that they were no longer going to pay for my clothing or haircuts. At first I was a little shocked—I thought I had done something wrong. But then they explained that they were just trying to help me learn to budget. (Although the meeting did seem to coincide with an incident in which my mom, fed up with me wearing my socks outside without shoes, said she would never buy me socks again!) They increased my monthly allowance, but not enough to support every item I desired. There was a gap between my needs and wants big enough that I had to fill it with my own money from babysitting.

My feelings of shock were quickly replaced by pride in my accomplishments. I was the only kid I knew who paid for her own haircuts. I thought it was cool. As soon as I could work, I began putting away half of every paycheck. By the time I was in college, I had a sizeable nest egg saved and was able to take a year off college to live in Spain. I've not quite lived up to those rigorous saving habits since, but I'm still proud that I put myself through college and paid for both of my cars on my own. Even when I wasn't executing so well in other areas of my life, I was always proud to pay my own way. And now, I know that for me it was and is important never to be dependent on a boyfriend/partner for money.

Remember, this parental intervention happened when Brooke was twelve—right at the stage when clothes are vitally important to a young girl and a desire for independence is emerging. Her parents shifted from a monotonous lecture on spending too much on clothes to giving her a hands-on experience with managing her needs and wants.

Brooke's financial journey wasn't flawlessly smooth ever after (what journey is?), but she counts this learning experience as one of the great financial opportunities of her young life. And what I took from this story was her parents' *readiness* to be financial mentors.

Giving kids a financial apprenticeship means being ready to say the same thing a thousand times ("Just because you can, doesn't mean you should," "You

can have a car when you're ready to manage the expenses that go with a car,"
"You can have a credit card as long as you commit to doing what it takes to
build and keep a credit score of 750 or better") and hanging in when it's hard.
In this case, Brooke's parents interpreted "taking care of their daughter" as
helping her to stretch—a key part of instilling sound financial skills and values.
They didn't ease up on her when she performed well; indeed, the stakes got
progressively higher over time. By the time she was old enough to buy her own
car, she both expected to do that and was proud that she could.

Setting the bar high enough for kids to grow while not setting it so high
that they check out—feeling overwhelmed and defeated before they begin—is
a key part of the parental high-wire act. You will find the Life/Money Maps
throughout this book helpful in this regard. But it's worth keeping in mind
that a child's capability often does exceed his parents' expectations.

Moving On

Now that you have a framework for launching the financial apprenticeship, let's
vanquish some "money monsters" that may try to impede your progress.

"If consumer society has one Achilles' heel . . . it is that consumer society doesn't make us unbelievably happy."

BILL MCKIBBEN,
AMERICAN JOURNALIST

Outwitting the
Money Monsters

Even if you are a model parent with a firm grasp of your own financial responsibilities, there are daunting money monsters poised to challenge your authority as a financial mentor and intent on speeding your kids along the highway of spending and consumption. Here are the top four monsters:

1. Time: For most families there is little to spare.
2. Peers: The influence of children's friends can be more powerful than that of family.
3. Media and marketing: The point of advertising is to convince consumers—especially children—to *want* and to *indulge,* sabotaging your best efforts and tempting kids into the vast bazaar of the material world.
4. Magical thinking: From the tooth fairy to ATMs that spit out money like magic, kids get mixed messages about the reality of money.

Money Monster I: Time

Let's face it, there is never enough time. Whether you have a staff of five or *are* a staff of five, every day comes to a close with a list of unfinished to-dos. And even as this book encourages you to raise financially fit kids, hundreds of other books want you to pay attention to improving children's reading skills, being conscious of physical fitness, or nurturing musical talents. Parents are bombarded with "must-dos." My aim is to help you become a better money mentor for your children while getting you to bed earlier.

Creating a Money Mentoring Team

One way to compensate for lack of time is the creation of a money mentoring team—delegating to get more time for yourself and real help for the kids. Think of this as a sanity network, a team to support both you and your kids. The team should include friends, relatives, or acquaintances who

- Are comfortable talking about and managing their own money
- Have some special expertise or unique knowledge
- Can give two to three days a year to host children at their place of work, or engage them in some activity that has a financial or economic focus (you can also just give friends and relatives a copy of this book and suggest they offer one activity a year from it!)
- You feel at ease and open with (otherwise they will not be a good sanity network for you)

Young people report it's easier for parents to discuss drugs and sex with them than to discuss money—which is to say that the conversations rarely happen. Building a money mentoring team is one way to get the subject on the table and into the real lives of the next generation. To create the team, think about your social capital:

- Has your sister or brother assembled a respectable nest egg?
- Do you have a friend who raises money for nonprofits and can shed light on the economics of philanthropy?
- Do you know anyone who works in mortgage loans or commercial credit? Ask them to let your teenager accompany them on a visit to a house being sold and talk about how the mortgage process works.

- How about the parent you met at the last PTA meeting who mentioned she's in charge of making sure her company's benefits are family-friendly? Ask her to explain to your college senior what a family-friendly benefit is. If a face-to-face meeting is too much to ask, an email, letter, or video would work.
- Think about successful entrepreneurs you know. Invite them to dinner and ask them to describe their life choices. Encourage them to tell stories: how they started, what the challenges were, and what they wish they had known earlier.
- Do you have a friend who teaches in public school or neighbors who work in city government, the fire department, or the police force? A quick lesson in local economics is a civic lesson for kids who will one day pay taxes.

The idea is to find people with whom you can barter time. Ask them to spend a couple of days a year with your kids (a team of six can translate into twelve to eighteen days of money talk per year for your kids) and offer a service in return—maybe a gift certificate for a massage or a great bottle of wine would do the trick. This is a practical solution for making an apprenticeship sustainable.

Every family will create a different team. For one child you might call on your best friend, a grandparent, your investment advisor, and maybe an aunt and a coworker. For another, you might ask your dad, a coworker, and a favorite teacher. Whatever the makeup, the idea is to create an extended family of money mentors who will, over time, reinforce key ideas and expectations, offer a steady stream of money–skill-building experiences, and take the pressure off you as the only source of your children's financial education. Think of your team as part of that "village" it takes to raise a child.

Making the Team Work

One way to make the team effective is to make it formal. Talk with team members; be clear on the role you hope they will play in your children's lives. Give them a Money Mentor's Kit (a copy of *Raising Financially Fit Kids*, a short biography of your child, and a list of three to five key family money values) and a solid sense of what you hope they will focus on with your kids. But get their input, too. A good money mentor may be inventive in ways you have not yet thought of—and sometimes he or she will be led by your kids' specific interests. Here's a sample invitation for use with prospective team members.

Dear _____,

I'm recruiting a small group of friends and family to help us raise a financially fit child. You've come to mind because {you have a rapport with Simon; Bill and I respect the life choices you have made; your natural ability as a life teacher with kids is so evident; etc}. I am/we are prepared to return the favor in some equivalent way if you will join Simon's money mentoring team.

Let me bring you up to date on Simon, who is now eleven and in the fifth grade. He plays soccer and is a fair-to-good student. We're trying to be conscious about the money skills and values we help Simon develop so he will become an independent, financially responsible adult. We hope that an active team of caring role models and resources will have a collective impact that will serve him well in this process.

If you will spend four to ten hours with Simon over the course of a year (a couple of afternoons or a Saturday morning—whatever works in your schedule), it will make a big contribution to helping him become independent and financially thoughtful. I've enclosed a Money Mentor's Kit that offers some ideas to get you started if you agree to accept this invitation. But please trust your own instincts as well. Whether you'd like to share a breakfast discussion of how you started your own career or suggestions on how to manage an allowance, I'm inviting you to join our team because I know Simon will benefit from spending time with you by informally developing his financial values and skill.

Obviously such a commitment warrants a trade on our part. I know that you love the theater. How about season tickets to the Great White Way Repertory Company {or an exquisite bottle of wine, or tickets to a baseball game, or . . . }?

If this is agreeable, I will introduce the two of you and leave it to you to get started. I look forward to hearing from you soon.

Sincerely,

Cynthia A. Parent

How a mentor spends time with your kids will depend on the age of the child and the interests of the mentor. But to alleviate any fears potential mentors may have that you are expecting a graduate-level day with your kids, suggest some of the activities offered in the following chapters, as well as a few of these:

Suggested Money Mentor's Kit

Raising Financially Fit Kids

Ten Basic Money Skills bookmark

Biography of your child

List of three to five family money values

- Go to lunch or breakfast and discuss how, when, and why (as well as why not) to buy things such as cars, computers, DVD players, and houses on credit.

- Share your own story of financial independence: how and why you started your company, chose your career, bought your first home (or car), or selected the financial plan you now rely on.

- Spend time together surfing financial sites; talk about what they do and why they're important. (Suggestions for websites can be found in the Life/Money Maps in Part Two of this book.)

- Take teens along to observe a financial transaction (negotiating the purchase of a car; leasing space for a horse, buying a large appliance, making a significant donation).

- Send a letter (one that actually arrives in the mail) sharing your thoughts or ideas about saving, spending, and giving money away.

Reassure the team they are not expected to teach your kids *everything* about money and financial responsibility. This is, after all, a drip, drip, drip process. The simple experience of spending time with them gives kids the opportunity to absorb, observe, and experience aspects of an adult's real financial life.

Kimberley Clouse, one of the world's great aunts and money mentors, shared this story:

> For Christmas I gave my niece an ATM bank, available online for about $30, to teach her that money doesn't just automatically appear when you go to the ATM—you have to actually deposit money to have money. After she received the gift, we talked about how it worked: if you have $30 in your ATM bank, and want to take out $10 to buy a doll, how much would you have left? She was learning simple math while discovering that the ATM was not a magical source of money, but a simple machine that functioned like a

big calculator. This activity flowed wonderfully into more conversations about ways to earn the money to deposit in the ATM bank. I am trying to instill a consciousness of her own entrepreneurial spirit in our time together. Another of my favorite birthday and Christmas gifts is a budget. It sounds a little strange, but she doesn't just get money to spend any way she likes; she also gets a money lesson—and believe me, she does not forget the gift or the lesson. The first time we did this I gave her $30 to spend—which she thought sounded like a lot!—until we went shopping and she realized how much most toys cost.

Aunts and uncles make great money mentors because their bond with the child is often deep enough to warrant a high degree of trust, yet distant enough that they are experienced as "cool" in a way parents rarely are.

Money Monster 2: Peers

"But Mooooommm, everyone has one."

"What's wrong with it? Everyone wears it this way."

"Come on, the whole class is going to . . ."

These classic whines recur in various forms, generation after generation. The power of peers to influence kids—for better and worse—is a reality to deal with when it comes to money issues. Judith Rich Harris, author of *The Nurture Assumption*, maintains that genes predispose children to develop a certain kind of personality, "but the environment can change them . . . not the environment their parents provide—but the outside-the-home environment, the environment they share with their peers." According to Harris, that effect starts as early as three years of age and can show up in nursery school.

When *The Nurture Assumption* was first published, it was greeted with skepticism—flying in the face, as it did, of the conventional wisdom that kids were most influenced by nature (genes) or nurture (parents). Harris may not be the last word on what most influences children, but it is hard to argue about the effect of your children's friends on their behavior and attitudes. I was reminded of this fact by a parent who told me the following story:

Five-year-old Kari lost a tooth and, on the instruction of her grandmother, put it under her pillow. "The tooth fairy collects those things," the grandmother said, "and will give you something special in return." The next morning Kari looked under her pillow and, sure enough, there was a fresh $5 bill.

That afternoon Kari was playing with her friend Lesley and announced that the tooth fairy had brought her $5 the previous night. Lesley had recently lost a tooth too, but her tooth fairy had left her only $1. Lesley could already discern that she had gotten a lesser deal than Kari and ran to her mom to demand why. Taken aback, the mom couldn't come up with a good explanation, but the next time Lesley lost a tooth, the tooth fairy had gotten the message and increased her contribution. Clearly, tooth fairies in the neighborhood realized they were dealing with some valuable teeth!

Down the street, four-year-old Linda's mom began to hear about the acts of the tooth fairy and decided things were getting out of hand when a fairy could set an inflated price on a baby tooth hardly big enough to see. After a call to Kari's grandmother and a little heart-to-heart with Lesley's mom and a few other parents, they all agreed to contract with just one tooth fairy—the one who gave only $1 for a tooth.

Moral of the story for kids: don't blab if you're lucky enough to get a generous tooth fairy! Moral of the story for parents: share the financial apprenticeship stage with other parents, discussing standards and values and dilemmas.

Parental isolation contributes to the power of peers—and financial anarchy among kids. When parents aren't talking to one another, kids rule. And rites of passage have become more elaborate and extravagant (bar and bat mitzvahs, sweet sixteen parties, proms, and first cars), with the most outrageous being turned into prime-time reality TV. Unfortunately, parents often succumb to what's easy, leaving kids in charge. And worldly though today's kids may be, they are not necessarily wise.

Kids do not have the monopoly on social media. Parents can connect through school networks, personal networks, and Facebook to break out of the parental isolation that is so harmful to their kids. Whether talking to parents on your son's soccer team or checking in with parents in your daughter's sixth-grade class, you defuse the power of your kids' peer expectations by agreeing on a few basic behaviors you will enforce *en masse* as parental peers. Being the first parent to speak up and say "I can't (or don't want to) spend $3,000 on my son's prom expenses or $50,000 on my daughter's bat mitzvah or $25,000 on a new car" may be tough, and not all parents will appreciate your efforts. But it just may be a strategy for creating a more evolved financial consciousness among your child and his friends.

Another strategy to employ is to embrace the power of peers—co-opting, rather than fighting it. Want to get a point across about saving or spending money? Create a group experience in which your children and their peers get the message together. For example, if the after-school gathering spot is a fast-food hangout and your daughter is worried she'll be left out if she doesn't show up, no amount of sermonizing on how she is wasting money on empty calories will be effective in changing her behavior. Rather, try an activity that teaches budgeting through a Scavenger Hunt for your daughter and her friends or setting up a lunch for your son and his buddies with a friend who has started a company and is willing to talk about what it took to start the business. Here is one way to engage your kids' friends without alienating your children.

Mall Scavenger Hunt

Scavenger Hunt Rules	Sample List of Items to Locate and Photograph
1. Point of the game: be the team to spend the least money on the most imaginative solutions to the hunt.	Something you would need at a rock concert
	An overnight bag for a trip to Paris
	Down pillows for a bedridden aunt
2. You have ninety minutes to find and document your solutions.	An MP3 player or tablet for listening to music
	Ingredients for a picnic with four friends
	Something with which to entertain a four-year-old
3. Be ready to defend your choices and give detailed info to the judges, who can give up to ten points for each solution.	Something to help your big brother lose weight
	An alarm clock that guarantees you will always wake up on time for class
4. The team with the most points wins.	A toy for a cat and a toy for a dog
	A birthday gift for a great teacher

Like it or not, going to the mall is twenty-first-century recreation. Shopping is entertainment. And exhorting kids to *not* consume excessively is less effective than helping them make that decision on their own. This Mall Scavenger Hunt is designed to help them become conscious about how and where they spend money. It requires a little setup time, but the payoff is worth it.

Ask your son or daughter and their best friend to invite six to twelve kids for a Mall Scavenger Hunt. On the day of the party, organize the kids into teams of three or four each and hand each team a digital camera (if they don't have a smartphone; the idea is to have instant results), the Scavenger Hunt list, and $500 of play money (raid those old board games you haven't played in years, or purchase stacks of fake cash at a local toy store).

The aim of this hunt is to be the team that brings home photos of the most imaginative solutions for the least cost. Once they have instructions, drive or send them (depending on their age) to the local mall or your town's main street. Give each group ninety minutes to collect photos of the items on the list and agree to meet at a specific time (points are deducted if a team is late). Have them display their photos and defend their solutions to earn points.

You can repeat this once a month, working up to a grand tournament. Skills and innovation will increase over time.

Financial Film Festival

Like the Mall Scavenger Hunt, the purpose of a Financial Film Festival is to engage kids and their peers in an informed conversation about money, values, and dreams. Set it up as an after-school or weekend event: one movie each month, with popcorn and a money mentor team member to discuss the movie with the kids. (For movie suggestions, see the sidebar.)

Questions worth posing for the films include

- What does this story have to do with money?
- What financial values do the characters portray?
- How do the characters reflect or stand at odds with your own values?
- What touched you in the story? What made you sad, angry, envious, joyful . . . ?
- What lessons about money and people can you take from the film?
- How does the film connect to current events? To history? To the future?
- What do you wish you could tell the characters to do?

Financial Film Festival

Baby Mama

Boiler Room

Moneyball

The Social Network

The Perfect Game

Maxed Out

Mildred Pierce

Sweet Smell of Success

It's a Wonderful Life

Searching for Superman

Money Book Club

A Town Like Alice, Nevil Shute

What You Owe Me, Bebe Moore Campbell

The Dollmaker, Harriette Louisa Simpson Arnow

20 $ecrets to Money and Independence: The DollarDiva's Guide to Life, Joline Godfrey

Pride and Prejudice, Jane Austen

The Merchant of Venice, William Shakespeare

A Room of One's Own, Virginia Woolf

The Hunger Games, Suzanne Collins

Let My People Go Surfing, Yvon Chouinard

The $100 Start-Up, Chris Guillebeau

See Goodreads for more suggestions: bit.ly/IMI _ goodreads

Money Book Club

What you are trying to do is instill a consciousness of financial responsibility. A Money Book Club is one way to achieve that. Invite five or six parent/child teams (if you like, this can be structured as a father/son or mother/daughter event) to meet once a month or once a quarter to discuss a book with themes related to money, finance, economics, and values. You don't have to use dry economic texts—there are a lot of riveting books that will do the trick: from Michael Lewis's *Moneyball* to Kathryn Stockett's *The Help*. Both fiction and nonfiction are powerful ways to engage the brain and sentiment of the next generation. (See the sidebar for more reading suggestions.) Local authors are often happy to speak to book clubs, so if there's someone you'd like to interview in person, go ahead and call, email, or write.

The Charity Café

Altruism emerges early in kids. Channeling their urge to "do good" is easy with the Charity Café. Invite six friends for a night at the Charity Café. The idea is to have kids redirect money they would normally spend on a fast-food meal to something that will "make a difference." With twelve kids giving $5 or $10 each, they'll have up to $120 to give away at each meeting. Over time they will choose to save and give more in one place.

Set up the kitchen or living room with five or six big posters (see the chart for some charity ideas): one for animals, one for the environment, one for health-related issues, one for homeless children, and one or two blank posters kids can fill in themselves.

When the kids arrive, have them put their contributions in a Charity Café bowl and fix themselves a sandwich. Serve something simple (peanut butter and jelly or make-it-yourself subs), so more time and attention is spent on charity than on food. Invite the

Animal Charities	Environmental Charities	Health Charities
Humane Society	Sierra Club	Blood Bank
Cat/Dog Spaying Fund	Land Conservancy	Children's Hospital
Pet Adoption Center	Recycling Fund	Cancer Fund for Children
Animal Hospital	Surfrider Foundation	Ronald McDonald House
Rescue Dog Foundation	Botanical Garden	Soup Kitchen

kids to take a look at the posters and think about which of the listed charities they would like to see their money donated to that evening.

Then get the party started. Organize the group into three teams of four kids each. Give each team fifteen minutes to designate two charities they want to support. Once the teams have chosen, have them describe how and why they made their selections. Give the full group time to discuss each team's choices and then ask them to vote again as a whole.

Once the choices have been narrowed to the two top vote-getters, suggest that the kids do a web search (or call the organization and talk with them, or visit the library) to get more information on each of the groups they've selected. Let them know this is a normal part of the due diligence process. It's a concept they should address early in their effort to practice charitable giving. Then have them do one last vote to select the charity that will receive that night's contribution.

Finally, give each of the original teams an assignment: one team to take or send the money to the group selected, another team to select new charities to consider at the next Café meeting, and a third group to find and invite a philanthropist to talk at the next meeting (you can help them with this by providing suggestions and telephone numbers, or have the kids ask their parents to recommend a family friend who might be able to fill this role). The older the kids in the group, the faster you can cede control and management of the Charity Café to the kids themselves.

If the group gels and the kids stay involved, you'll find they will become increasingly sophisticated about their choices. For now, think of the Charity Café as just one way to engage children by engaging their peers.

Money Monster 3: Media and Marketing

In his sage (and still relevant) book *Fatherhood*, Bill Cosby observes: "A parent quickly learns that no matter how much money you have, you will never be able to buy your kids everything they want. You can take a second mortgage on your house and buy what you think is the entire Snoopy line: Snoopy pajamas, Snoopy underpants, Snoopy linen, Snoopy shoelaces, Snoopy cologne, and Snoopy soap, but you will never have it all. And if Snoopy doesn't send you to the poorhouse, Calvin Klein will direct the trip. Calvin is the slick operator who sells your kids things for eighty-five dollars that cost seven at Target."

And those slick operators he refers to get slicker all the time. Whether it's the college senior who is urged to "put this purchase on a Gap card and save 10 percent" (and risk lowering their FICO score) or the seemingly endless ways to spend virtual money and buy the latest app, there is no end of opportunities for kids to enter the material culture, thanks to the imaginative talent of twenty-first-century marketeers.

In fact, a new trend—the "freemium" business model—is spreading like wildfire in the app universe. Under this model, apps can be downloaded for free, but much of the content is driven by purchases that are made when using the app. Whether kids are urged to buy birthday presents for the animals in their virtual zoo or to pay to unlock the next level in the quest to save a kingdom, game developers are making enormous sums of money by charging users à la carte for the experience. Notice that I said game developers. This is because most in-app purchases are tied to games and therefore targeted at children. If you want to see for yourself how big this business is, just open the App Store or Google Play application and find the top free downloads. Most of these apps are free, meaning their revenue is generated entirely from purchases made while using the application.

Ten years ago, parents could rest assured that after they had bought the expensive video game console and game, their wallets would be safe while the kids saved the galaxy. However, the rocket ships of today's games need extra fuel and missiles, and of course the crew members need shiny new spacesuits— all of which are easily purchased through a simple tap on the screen. Defenders of this business model cite password protections on accounts linked to credit cards as a firewall to prevent accidental or unwanted purchases. However, the Web is rife with stories of parents bewildered at how their child could figure out their password (many of these parents are the same ones who proudly gush over how tech-savvy their children are) and dismayed that the $200 charge for a trunk full of stars, coins, or magic berries is nonrefundable. Suddenly this "free" app costs the equivalent of a week's worth of groceries.

On billboards, in the school cafeteria, on the Web, or at the local fast-food dive, "Buy me, buy me!" messages prevail. No parent has the resources to compete directly with the marketing genius of Facebook, Zynga, Google, and the yet-to-emerge next IPO giant. Whether you're up against the latest David Beckham–meets-H&M campaign or Justin Bieber selling perfume, in the face of such raw power, any attempt to get your kids to not spend so much money is, for the most part, an act of futility.

The good news is that, in addition to banding together with local parents to set standards, there are other antidotes to the daily bombardment your kids are exposed to.

Teach Kids to Question Television Authorities

Actively watching television with kids gives you a chance to offer a running quiz about the validity of claims made, the motives behind programs and messages, and the nature of the images shown. You don't need to turn your ten-year-old into a jaded cynic to help him think critically about the messages fed to him on TV. If you handle the task with humor and a light hand, kids soon sort out the real from the manipulative and make good decisions on their own.

Experiment with a Currency of Your Own

While retailers have been creating their own currencies to coax money out of your kids' pockets, over two hundred communities around the United States have created local currencies (Madison Hours, Ithaca Hours, Maine Time Dollars) to create ways for neighbors and community members to trade and barter with one another—or, as they put it in Maine, to "encourage the exchange of service credits . . . among neighbors and friends."

Madison Hours, for example, was initiated in 1996 in Madison, Wisconsin, to spur sustainable, grassroots economic development. As Camy Mathy reported in Yes magazine, she has bought "custom sewing, a felt hat, a printer for my computer, and garden seedlings." In my own community of Ojai, California, Bart's Books, a local bookstore, lets me trade my old books for new ones. I have a running account, save space on my own bookshelves, and can always afford to "buy" new books. In Ojai, books function as a kind of alternative currency. These alternative forms of money help kids understand the function of currency while giving them up-close-and-personal experiences using the currency in your community. For more information on community currencies, visit www.ithacahours.org, www.madisonhours.org, or www.mtdn.org.

Make Parental Connections on a Large Scale

A concerted effort on behalf of kids *can* be effective—we find proof of this in the success of such efforts as Mothers Against Drunk Driving; Vicki Abeles' film *Race to Nowhere*, which has caused schools nationwide to review their homework policies; and Lady Gaga's creation of the Born This Way Foundation, in partnership with the Berkman Center for Internet & Society, which has helped bring attention to the phenomenon of bullying among kids. These calls to action have resulted in networks, organizations, and resources that counter parental isolation in the face of powerful cultural forces that are at odds with personal values,

You can equip kids to think for themselves about the messages coming at them. As members of the most media-savvy generation in history, these kids do not buy everything they hear about. But they do need a clear set of values to power the internal compass they will use to make their own decisions about what's hot and what's not, what they need and what they don't. Think of these values as a kind of psychic armor your kids can use to defend themselves against the manipulations of the media.

Money Monster 4: Magical Thinking

Kids often get mixed messages about the easy availability of money. That's not surprising, when you think about the fairy tales that connect gold and magic. Of course, we want the world of children to be magical and full of wonder. What could be better than the look of joy on a four-year-old's face when she emerges in the morning, having found money under her pillow in exchange for a lost tooth? It's the same look of wonder a forty-five-year-old might have if he found a new Maserati in the driveway!

I'm not Scrooge, and I don't think it necessary to drain wonder from the lives of kids to make them financially responsible. However, it is important to be conscious of the messages we send, minimizing the connections we set up for them between wonder and awe—and money. The next time the tooth fairy visits, put a small toy or a movie ticket under your child's pillow, or a note with a promise to read a favorite book or take her on a special adventure. Whenever possible, try to separate money from magic. (If you would like to learn more about ways you can separate magical thinking from that little fairy who has a thing for enamel, see my blog post: http://bit.ly/joline_toothfairy.)

Another culprit is the ATM. When children are old enough to use it, make sure they understand that they're dealing with real money, from a real source. Open an account with a deposit that includes some of their own money from savings or earnings, then walk them through the process of taking some of that money out of the ATM, reading the account slip, and then calling the bank's toll-free number to confirm that their account balance has decreased.

Resources for Media Literacy

A media education resource for families, www.parentfurther.com/technology-media

Killing Us Softly, an updated documentary on gender representation in advertising by Jean Kilbourne, www.jeankilbourne.com

A PBS website teaching children to decipher media and advertising, http://pbskids.org/dontbuyit

The greatest disservice a parent can do—even if you can afford to—is to make a deposit, give your child an ATM card, and keep filling the well every time she runs out. The digital age is pretty magical, and by the time your six-year-old is ready to wave her digital fingertip to make a purchase, or look into an optic scan to withdraw money, the disconnect from the hard green stuff will be complete. When it comes to teaching kids about money, literal and concrete is good.

Raising financially fit kids isn't a mysterious process and needn't be overly taxing. If your goal is simply to raise a great kid (as opposed to, say, a teenage arbitrager), a modicum of attention to the basics we've just covered—money styles, money values, and the money monsters you are in a contest with—is about all you need to guide your kids through a financial apprenticeship. Moreover, if you assemble a loving and reliable money mentoring team, you won't have to make this journey alone.

In Part Two, The Financial Apprenticeship, I offer specific how-to's for countering money monsters and staying focused on this most critical part of your children's quest for independence.

Part Two

The Financial Apprenticeship

The Money Skills Map

I've pointed out some of the pressures children face on their financial journey.

The next five chapters introduce Ten Basic Money Skills that constitute the apprentice's financial tool kit. You will find activities tailored to five stages of the life cycle. This chart will be filled in chapter by chapter, offering specific activities for each age group and money skill.

Selecting from the activities will give you a personalized plan for your own family.

	Ages 5–8: I'm Just A Kid	**Ages 9–12:** Encouraging Passions
	Children are preoccupied with many developmental tasks during these years. In the context of their financial journey, this is the time to begin introducing basic financial language and values.	These are the years when you can piggyback on the unharnessed enthusiasm and curiosity of tweens. Demonstrate the links between pursuing passions and having the means to realize those passions, and between opportunity and responsibility.
Ten Basic Money Skills	**Actions (5–8)**	**Actions (9–12)**
1. How to save		
2. How to get paid what you're worth		
3. How to spend wisely		
4. How to talk about money		
5. How to live within a budget		
6. How to invest		
7. How to exercise the entrepreneurial spirit		
8. How to handle credit		
9. How to use money to change the world		
10. How to be a citizen of the world		

Ages 13–15: Breaking Away	Ages 16–18: Standing Tall	Ages 19+: It's Never Too Late
When it comes to money, these may be the most difficult and the most fruitful learning years. Young teens are dealing with the confusion of both wanting and fearing independence. These are the years to connect financial choices and consequences. In these years, true impact is possible.	These are the years when it all comes together—or you are hustling to play catch-up. Either way, now is the time when acquiring financial responsibility can go hand in hand with a new maturity.	As kids become adults they embark on meaningful independent experiences, often for the first time—work, college, public service, etc. Help them help themselves by giving them the means to learn what they need to know.
Actions (13–15)	**Actions (16–18)**	**Actions (19+)**

"Someone's sitting in the shade today because someone planted a tree a long time ago."

WARREN BUFFETT,

INVESTOR

Stage One
Ages 5–8: I'm Just a Kid

I once spoke to a group of financial advisors and asked them to describe things they do to pass on good financial habits to their youngest children. There were a lot of great ideas, but the most memorable was the dad who claimed he was teaching his six-year-old to calculate the time value of money. I am in favor of starting the financial apprenticeship early, but this may be overdoing it! Whatever money messages and skills you want to pass along to your kids must be done in the context of young attention spans and readiness.

Most five- to eight-year-olds are curious, literal, have high energy, and absorb information rapidly—shifting from subject, object to idea to experience in nanoseconds. How then to get them started on a journey of economic literacy that will last a lifetime?

The Life/Money Map
Stage One/Ages 5–8

Social/Emotional Development	Appropriate Money Skills to Master
Is curious	Counts coins and bills
Has short attention span	Understands the value and purpose of money
May have very high energy	Learns to differentiate between wants and needs
Begins to view fairness as important	Begins to develop an ethical compass

Big Tasks for Stage One

For this earliest stage of the financial apprenticeship there are six big tasks you can expect to accomplish:

1. Introduce the Ten Basic Money Skills.
2. Start an allowance.
3. Observe and respond to children's money styles as they begin to emerge.
4. Establish and communicate your family's financial vision to other family members, your mentoring team, friends, and your kids.
5. Begin a savings program with your kids. For very young children, even very small compound interest rates add up over time, and a grasp of the concept of compound interest is a pre-requisite to understanding how to invest once they have acquired savings and enough money to do so.
6. Calm yourself; calm your kids. Breathe.

By accomplishing these tasks, you give kids a sound introduction to the first stage of their apprenticeship.

1. Introducing the Ten Basic Money Skills

The money skills chart in the foldout offers a guide to activities and resources that are effective in this age range. Experiment—these activities won't fit every child, and you won't have time to do them all. Keep in mind that kids at this stage are impressionable and that one great experience can make a lasting impression.

An allowance is not an entitlement or a salary. It is a tool for teaching children how to manage money.

2. Starting the First Allowance: Trumping the Troublemaker

"But MaaaAAAAaaaa, it's my money; you can't tell me how to spend it."

"You can't make me clear the table for my allowance—I already made my bed, and that's all I have to do."

"Come on . . . I need more money—my allowance isn't enough."

"Everyone gets more money then I do—and they aren't expected to pay for their own school lunch either."

The allowance may be the most used and abused child-training tool ever devised—and the biggest family troublemaker. It begins when kids are very young and parents dole out a few dollars a week in an earnest attempt to begin teaching financial responsibility. Unfortunately, too often the kids end up training their parents how that allowance will be used. Little ones are so precocious!

We smile and chuckle over the child's attempts to be grown-up with her money. A quarter here, a dollar there, and soon her ability to hoodwink Mom, Dad, Grandpa, and Aunt Susie out of more money (because no one remembers what the allowance is really meant to cover) becomes apparent. And when that cute little tycoon morphs into a tyrant when frustrated by allowance rules, it's tempting to give her another dollar to stop the whining.

Flip Open

3. How to spend wisely	4. How to talk about money	5. How to live on a budget	6. How to invest
Start the conversation about "wants" and "needs" during a visit to a toy store or other intriguing destination. Before you arrive, decide on a small budget. Set parameters for how this money can be spent, and discuss the choices to be made—will it be spent all on one thing or on several smaller purchases? Create a budget for pet care. Ask your child to make choices to keep the total under a certain amount. Give your child a calculator when he shops with you so he can add the cost of purchases as you go. Teach your child to spell *discount*.	Young kids pick up language from TV and school friends. Make sure they hear financial values and terms from you. Talk about all the ways money is used. Discuss what food drives and homeless shelters are for. Never be afraid to say, "We can't afford it." Or "No." Never be afraid to say, "We can afford it, but this is not how I want to spend our money." Then explain why. Set up your first money-mentoring team.	Have kids count the money collected, earned, or spent each week and write it down on a chart. Make this a regular task, connected to some other routine (just before going on a walk with you or just after a warm bath) that helps it become automatic—and pleasurable. Remember, you are trying to unhook the issue of money from anxiety whenever possible. Start an allowance program (see page 52) around something she loves. Let her live with the consequences of exceeding her budget.	Invest in the future of you⋯ dren. Now may be the tim⋯ establish a 529 college sa⋯ plan for your kids' or gran⋯ education. Be aware of fe⋯ that can add substantial c⋯ to this investment vehicle⋯ Introduce the phrase *comp⋯ interest* and show your ch⋯ the numbers in his saving⋯ account passbook (on pap⋯ online) to illustrate how m⋯ makes money over time. Introduce the word *equity* (ownership): "I'll be an eq⋯ partner with you in a lemo⋯ stand." Explain that you'll⋯ vide the money for sugar a⋯ lemons and he will contrib⋯ sweat equity (the hard wo⋯ that way you'll share equit⋯ the business.
Alexander, Who Used to Be Rich Last Sunday, Judith Viorst *Money Doesn't Grow on Trees: Teaching Your Kids the Value of a Buck*, Ellie Kay *What Olivia Needs* coloring storybook, from the Nick Jr. show, bit.ly/NickJrOlivia	*Money Mama & The Three Little Pigs*, Lori Mackey *Save, Spend, or Donate? A Book About Managing Money*, Nancy Loewen and Brian Jensen *Pigs Will Be Pigs: Fun with Math and Money*, Amy Axelrod *The Monster Money Book*, Loreen Leedy	*The Berenstain Bears' Trouble with Money*, Stan Berenstain *If You Made a Million*, David M. Schwartz *Eyewitness: Money*, Joe Cribb	*Stock Market Pie*, J. M. Sey⋯ Resources for 529 plans: www.savingforcollege.com⋯ *Maisy Makes Lemonade*, ⋯ Cousins *Once Upon a Company . .⋯ A True Story*, Wendy Ande⋯ Halperin

...w to exercise the ...preneurial spirit	8. How to handle credit	9. How to use money to change the world	10. How to be a citizen of the world
...rage entrepre-...l projects ...nade stands, ...all card stands). ...our child deter-...what to charge for ...cts or services. ...your child when ...ercises her ...preneurial muscle ...enterprising!" ...resourceful!"). ...e a kitchen gallery ...ng entrepreneur-...e models. ...stories of social ...preneurs: the ...thropist pastor ...tarts a youth ...e organization, ...crofinancier, and	Make a big deal about trust. Refer to it ("I trust you"); explain it ("Trust is how you know Dad and I will make sure you have breakfast every morning"); require it ("I want to trust you to cross the street only when the light says to"). Help your child get his first library card and explain that it's like a credit card. You borrow a book, it is noted on your library account with a due date, and if you return it late or not at all, you have to pay. Let kids borrow small amounts of money from you; make them pay it back from their allowance. (Be sure to teach the basics of paying back debts promptly, not getting into debt.) If you buy something for your kid on your credit card, show him the bill when it comes in and explain how you must pay for the item now.	Each week, set aside a portion of their allowance in a giving jar. Once a quarter, let them decide where to donate it. At Thanksgiving, have kids put cans of food into food drive bins (ask them to buy at least one of the cans with money from their "give away" fund). At Christmas or Chanukah, make sure kids contribute to a gift collection for children who are in the hospital or homeless. Create a family day on which everyone gives a half-day of volunteer work to a local nonprofit or community project. Keep a running list of all the things you do to help others posted where kids can see it. Talk about why you do it.	A foreign currency scrapbook offers tangible evidence that although money is global, how it is expressed is local. The path to their minds starts with their mouths. Expand their palates with international cuisine.
...he Second Grade ...,205.50 to Visit ...atue of Liberty, ...n Zimelman et al. *...Jed's Barbershop*, ...ree King Mitchell	*Being Trustworthy: A Book About Trustworthiness*, Mary Small *Neale S. Godfrey's Ultimate Kids' Money Book*, Neale S. Godfrey	*Imagine If . . . I Could Calm a Storm*, Kathy Speight, Camden Speight, and Janis Acampora *Those Shoes*, Maribeth Boelts and Noah Z. Jones *Cloud Tea Monkeys*, Mal Peet, Elspeth Graham, Juan Wijngaard *Littlejim's Gift*, Gloria Houston *Sam and the Lucky Money*, Karen Chinn	*The Kids' Multicultural Cookbook (Kids Can!)*; Deanna F. Cook offers kid-friendly recipes from around the world, lightly peppered with fun facts.

How you live your life

is central to what you will teach

your kids about money.

An allowance is not a salary or

an entitlement. It is a tool for teaching

children how to manage money.

Introducing the Ten Basic Money Skills

This chart is a guide to activities and resources effective in this age range. Experiment with these activities and ideas—they won't all fit your child, and you won't have time to do them all. Keep in mind that kids at this stage are very impressionable—great expectations can make big impressions.

	Basic Money Skill	
	1. How to save	**2. How to get paid what you're worth**
Actions: 5–8 Years	Present a piggy bank or money box (see Resources) as a rite of passage, and use a special envelope to give them an allowance each week. Talk about the things we save: money, old clothes to give away, "the day," for a rainy day. What do these phrases mean and why do we use them? Visit a bank and open a savings account. Stop by frequently to deposit allowance or gift money. Teach your child how to spell *savings*.	Post a list of household jobs and a range of fees each job is worth. (These should be special assignments and not the everyday chores that everyone pitches in to complete.) Once a week, each child must choose one job and negotiate a payment amount. Make sure it's clear that the harder the job, the more it's worth. For these special projects, pay for time rather than assigning a flat fee—but make sure a time frame is agreed to ahead of time so she doesn't prolong the task to get paid extra! Start a library of "dream books"—stories about people who make money, do good, and have fun.
Resources	You can order kid-friendly "moneyboxes" at www.moonjar.com. *Rock, Brock, and the Savings Shock*, Sheila Bair and Barry Gott *The Money Tree Myth: A Parents' Guide to Helping Kids Unravel the Mysteries of Money*, Gail Vaz-Oxlade http://www.practicalmoneyskills.com/games/peterpigs/	*Money-Savvy Kids*, J. Raymond Albrektson *A Day's Work*, Eve Bunting *A Job for Jenny Archer*, Ellen Conford *Farmer's Market: Families Working Together*, Marcie R. Rendon *Doggone Lemonade Stand!*, Judy Bradbury

Now, pay attention. Here is an important mantra, best learned when the child is at his or her youngest and cutest stage (and when you are most susceptible to clever manipulation by the little sweetie):

An allowance is not an entitlement or a salary. It is a tool for teaching children how to manage money. It's money that gives children an opportunity to practice the Ten Basic Money Skills.

Say it again, with conviction: An allowance is not an entitlement or a salary. It is a tool for teaching children how to manage money. It's money that gives children an opportunity to practice the Ten Basic Money Skills.

If you decide to institute an allowance (and yes, it's a good idea), this is the message you must internalize and communicate. Just as blocks are great tools for developing motor skills, an early allowance develops money skills (saving, sharing, earning, counting) that will impact the rest of their lives. To help everyone remember, print this out in large type and stick it on your refrigerator.

> *Dear_____,*
> *Your allowance is not an entitlement or a salary. It's money you will use to practice the Ten Basic Money Skills; a tool to help you learn how to manage money.*
> *Love, Mom and Dad*

The first allowance begins with short, simple rules like these communicated often and clearly:

- An allowance helps you become a big, independent girl/boy.
- The better you handle money, the more quickly you will get additional responsibilities, privileges, and a bigger allowance to practice with.
- You will practice counting, earning, saving, sharing, growing, and spending.
- Every few months, we'll look at how you're doing with these skills and see what changes have been earned.

Managing the Allowance

At the first hint that you're dealing with an emerging labor negotiator (with all due respect to those professionals!) or that an attitude of entitlement is creeping in, rescind part or all of the allowance and start over with your mantra: *An allowance is not an entitlement or a salary. It's a tool for teaching children how to manage money.* Keep this clear and you'll have fewer arguments about money in the household because everyone will know the rules. Here are a few scenarios to help you out.

Scenario 1: Six-year-old Natasha gets $6 per week from her mom and dad as her first allowance. "Can I spend this any way I want?" asks Natasha. The most effective answer is:

a. "Of course, sweetie, it's your money."

b. "No, you'll have to get our okay before you spend anything."

c. "This is your learning money. This is money you will use to practice how to save and spend wisely. Your job is to practice doing those things well."

The answer is c: "This is your learning money." Remember, teaching kids to manage money developmentally is iterative. You will, over the years, repeat and repeat your themes. And though you may fear you're driving your kids crazy, they will learn and remember.

To make your message concrete (especially critical for the five- to eight-year-old), place three jars, cans, boxes, or other containers on a shelf with your child's name on the side of each: "Sam's Savings," "Sam's Money to Spend," "Sam's Money to Give to Causes." Have Sam count the money with you and then determine how much should go into each can. The amounts will vary with each family, reflecting financial values. Easy formulas are best when your children are very young: a third for each category. The rules you establish must apply to all money that comes Sam's way, whether it's birthday money from Grandma, a few dollars for a chore you ask him to do, or some form of financial serendipity.

Young children have not yet developed the sophistication to analyze money in complex ways. All they know is that it's cash and it came to them. If you do not have one rule that applies to all money when kids are very young, you will be negotiating with über–financial analysts when they are twelve. Some kids will be ready for this practice at four, but that may be too early for others—don't stress over a year or two. The point is to start with financial messages early—whatever that means in your family.

Is this harsh? Shouldn't children be able to enjoy the money that loving grandparents bestow? Can't birthday money be "exempt"? Of course, but be wary of communicating that money is handed out freely or of giving mixed messages. At this earliest stage your goal is to set expectations, establish boundaries, and communicate values. There are a lot of ways to demonstrate love to kids without opening wallets indiscriminately.

Scenario 2: Six-year-old Zoe has agreed to pick up her toys daily for a dollar-a-week increase in her allowance. This is:

a. A good way to introduce her to paid work

b. An incentive to encourage tidiness

c. A signal that being part of a family is a paid activity

d. A bad idea

The answer is d: "A bad idea." Whether you have live-in staff to manage your household or struggle to make ends meet, the function of a family is to love, live, and work together. There are obligations and privileges that must be shared. Well-meaning parents who pay for beds made, dishes cleared, or toys and equipment stored properly are later puzzled when, as they get older, the same kids tend not to "pull together" as part of the family unit. Raise your daughter's allowance if she is handling her three money jars well and you've discussed how the extra dollar will be used. Pick some "special chores" that warrant earned income if you like. But don't tie an allowance to performing tasks that should be part of family life. Of course you want to offer ways for kids to earn money in legitimate (not silly) ways. You might, for example, pay them to make *your* bed, but never their own—that's part of personal responsibility; you might pay for polishing silver (does anyone do that anymore?), but not for setting the table; you can pay for sorting coins, but not for putting their toys away. The rule of thumb is this: pay for anything you might hire someone else to do for *you*; don't pay for anything that helps them develop personal responsibility. Homes with help (nannies or housekeepers) should counsel those helpers to be part of the money mentoring team.

Scenario 3: Seven-year-old Matt has been faithfully putting his money into his three money jars for two years. The cash in his "spending jar" as well as his "giving money away" jar has been growing because, as a hoarder, he didn't want to let go of any of the cash. You think it's great he's turning into such a little saver. But by now the money adds up to several hundred dollars and you want him to open a bank account (a great chance to introduce compound interest and "making money while you sleep"). "No!" he screams. "I want it in my room!" You say:

a. "OK, it's your money after all."

b. "An allowance is meant for you to learn how to manage your money. Hoarding it in cans shows you aren't learning yet. We'll go to the bank in the morning and then start again."

c. "You won't get any more money until you agree to put what you have in the bank."

The answer is b. By telling kids they can do anything they want with their money (hoarding, spending in silly ways, keeping it under the mattress), you abdicate your mentoring role. And by threatening to withhold future money, you get yourself into a tug of wills that is usually counter-productive. You're the grown-up. Take the child to the bank—but don't go when one of you is cranky. Wait until you can go together in a sunny mood and combine the trip with a walk, some time spent in the park, or a bicycle ride. These are imprinting moments—stories that will be told to their kids decades from now.

Scenario 4: Aunt Meg has come for a visit that coincides with six-year-old Anna's birthday. She gives her a really cute dress and a card that has $30 inside. With a gleam in her eye, little Anna says, "Thank you, Aunt Meg! Will you take me to the store now?" You say:

a. "That sounds like fun. Let's all go together!"

b. "What a wonderful gift! Show Aunt Meg how you budget your money—she'll be so proud of you!"

c. "Now Anna, you know we agreed that all the money you get in gifts goes to your savings account."

The answer is b. Encouraging kids to spend money as soon as they get it reinforces the idea that holding on to it isn't important. But withholding a gift is a little hard-hearted. By encouraging her to treat the money as she always does, you reinforce the idea that *all* money must be managed for saving, spending, and giving away. Once part of the cash gift from Aunt Meg is in the savings jar and another part in the sharing jar, the part that goes into the spending jar can be used in a celebratory way, if Anna chooses.

Guidelines for Managing the Allowance

The following allowance guidelines are relevant at each stage of the financial apprenticeship and will help you navigate the tricky waters of kids and money.

Manage in the context of your goals. Are you trying to teach budgeting skills? Are you hoping to encourage independence? Allowances are less about financial transactions and more about the learning opportunities they afford. Decide what lessons you want to instill and then build the allowance plan around those lessons. Be clear about what you expect your child to learn and then hold her to those expectations.

Do not use the allowance for behavioral control. Money anxiety is deeply embedded in our psyches. Connecting an allowance to emotional or behavioral control exacerbates this and doesn't do much to help the child develop healthy financial habits. (I watch grown men and women cower at the very idea of dealing with their money because it triggers some deep, dark primal fear in their memory banks!) Using the allowance to reward or punish behavior distracts children from the main task of learning the Ten Basic Money Skills.

Remember the allowance is a tool, not an end in itself. Every year the allowance should be a little bigger and carry additional responsibility. If your eight-year-old gets $10 per week for trading cards and savings, when she's nine she should get $12 and be expected to pay for whatever her collectible is, set aside savings, and set aside money for a charity. You may want to put your fifteen-year-old on a monthly budget if he's mastered the weekly responsibility of an allowance. But if fourteen-year-old Dylan hasn't learned to save money from his allowance yet, or nine-year-old Maya can't count change properly, don't increase financial privileges until the financial responsibility commensurate with that age or stage has been mastered.

Institute a rite of passage. A rite-of-passage birthday dinner can help with this. The night before the actual birthday, take the child out to dinner—just the immediate family. This is not a time to divert attention to other kids. Focus. This should be a formal, fancy place: white tablecloths and the whole deal. No Chuck E. Cheese on this night—that's fine for the next day. We're going for gravitas the night before. (If you are economizing, organize dinner at home as if for company.)

And yes—do this with six- and seven-year-olds. They get it. While you're waiting for the appetizer to arrive, it's time to deliver a short speech that goes something like, "Darling, tomorrow is your birthday. And it's going to be *lots* of fun—cool presents, a great party, a huge celebration of how happy we are you are alive and part of this family! But *tonight*, we're going to talk about the responsibilities that go with being another year older."

With this simple declaration, you balance privilege with responsibility, fun and games with gratitude. What "another year older" actually means will be different in each family. In some it may be as simple as being kinder to a sibling; for others, setting the table or feeding the dog as a means of contributing to the family or adding a little more to the piggy bank or volunteering in the community. And for every child it can be a new responsibility associated with the allowance: saving more, giving more, increasing responsibility. It is different by age and family. But it is a powerful message, telling kids that growing up brings both new privileges (staying up or out later, acquiring greater independence) and new responsibilities.

Full disclosure: the first year you institute this rite of passage, your kids may blow you off (*just another dumb idea from parents*); the second year you repeat the dinner, they may roll their eyes (*here they go again*); but by the fourth and fifth years, if you're consistent and hang in, the pre-birthday dinner will be the new normal in your family—a tradition your kids may pass along to their kids. And it will make the expectations of balancing privilege with responsibility a lot easier to communicate for the rest of the year.

Tailor financial categories to your children. Some families include a college savings category; others include a favorite sport or hobby. If your daughter has horse fever, making her contribute to her passion will help her decide how serious she is. Categories also help reinforce values. If your family tithes to your religious affiliation, setting that goal early will send the message that it's an expectation. Starting a college fund for your child to contribute to, no matter how small, sends the message that college is a goal you hope he will pursue. And if you institute a college investing fund (like a 529, for example), you have the added advantage of an investment lesson.

There is no right amount. I'm often asked "How much should we give our kids for an allowance?" Rule of thumb is to start small and increase the allowance as the child's ability to manage responsibility increases. If she's always borrowing against the next week, you may want to back up and help her manage smaller amounts—or take another look at the real budget and expectations of what the allowance is intended to cover. The point is to learn how to manage money, not to cultivate high finance.

Remember that the allowance is yet another means to reinforce family financial values. The categories you stress, the expectations you are explicit about, and the consistency of your attention to the allowance and its management will communicate your financial beliefs. Don't miss this center-stage opportunity to highlight your family's core values.

I bought each of my five children everything up to a Rainbow Brite Jacuzzi and still I kept hearing "Dad, can I get . . . Dad, can I go . . . Dad, can I buy . . ." Like all other children, my five have one great talent: they are gifted beggars. Not one of them ever ran into the room, looked up at me, and said, 'I'm really happy that you're my father, and as a tangible token of my appreciation here's a dollar.' If one of them had ever done this, I would have taken his temperature."
—Bill Cosby, *Fatherhood*

---

3. Observing Money Styles

Remember the money styles referred to in chapter 1? How kids handle an allowance reflects their money style and gives clues about how to mitigate its dark side. Let's revisit those styles in the context of your five- to eight-year-old.

The hoarder. Because a child is under ten is no reason to underestimate his financial tenacity. Often the hoarder has figured out that holding tightly to money is a sure way to gain approval from Mom and Dad. Kids who figure out that saving equals parental approval will cover up a lot of other financial shenanigans with the chorus, "But gee, look how much I saved!" Although saving is one of the Ten Basic Money Skills we want to teach, hoarding is not. If the hoarder chooses to put 70 percent of his money into his savings jar and only 15 percent in each of his other money jars, that's fine—he's still learning the concept of *managing* money. To move things along, plan a special outing to spend the money on something of value or make a contribution to the Humane Society or a Children's Hospital. Be concrete and active, and emphasize to your hoarder that the point of the money is to manage it, not just hold on to it.

The spendthrift. Young children may be captivated by the magic of exchanging money for "stuff." Spending money for the first time is a powerful act for a child who often feels "small"—and the adrenaline surge that some people experience when they spend money can be hard to resist. Helping children feel powerful in other ways won't immediately curtail the urge to spend money, but making them conscious of their behavior is one way to manage it. The Ten Basic Money Skills activities are designed to help kids feel the competency that is so crucial to a sense of well-being. The spendthrift is essentially a child out of control, and that inner sense of being out of control never feels good. Helping children find ways to use spending habits as a means of acquiring discipline and self-confidence is an important aspect of your work at this point.

Before your next trip to the mall, have the spendthrift make a list of things he wants to buy. Let him know how much money you will allow him to budget ($5 to $50), then let him shop and help him add up what he's gathered. Compare this figure with how much money he holds. Has he stayed within the budget? If not, ask him to return the items he needs/wants the least. By putting him in control of money decisions, not just spending, you'll give him early practice in decision making—and increase his sense of personal power.

The scrimper. The scrimper may get real pleasure from coming home with change, and most parents will be wise not to tamper with such behavior. But if the scrimper also shows signs of withholding or selfish behavior with friends and family, it may be time to focus on the art of giving. As contributions to the "money to give away" jar accumulate, help your child select an activity or project to which she can dedicate the money. Set up a fund in her name at a local children's museum, or build a relationship with a science museum where she enjoys going and can see her money at work. You can ask the museum's development director to meet with your child and thank her for her contribution; this will help make the connection more concrete and give her a sense of pride in having done something generous. In this way you can help your little scrimper see how money can be used for pleasure when put to work wisely.

The giver. Between the ages of five and eight, it is unlikely this behavior will show itself to any great extent—this is a highly egocentric stage of life, and altruism may be nascent. But if you have a child who shows signs of a constant need for approval and who discerns that giving things away (toys, kisses, pictures) is a sure route to being liked, you may be getting early clues to keep an eye on as she grows older. We never want to discourage the generosity of a giving heart, but sometimes there can be a fine line between a genuine desire to give and approval-seeking behavior.

The beggar. "Can I? Can I?" is one of the most easily learned games in a child's repertoire. Usually it gets more pronounced over time as its success as a tactic for acquiring cash grows. Who has not given in to the game of "Can I?" just to make the sound go away? Next time, try one of these responses:

a. "I love you, and I really like to make you happy, but 'Can I?, Can I?' isn't a good way to get my attention. Think about what you want and how else you might help me understand how important it is to you."

b. "No."

c. "Tell me how this fits into the budget we worked on last week."

All of these responses are fine—the important thing is to make sure you do not reinforce the "Can I?" game, which gets increasingly unattractive and self-defeating as the child grows older.

The hustler. To think of an innocent five- to eight-year-old as a hustler is almost inconceivable. Yet the child who bargains for "just another ten minutes before I go to bed . . ." or who wheedles $20 out of his mom for a game his dad said he couldn't have or who tries to increase her allowance on a regular basis without real cause, is developing early negotiating skills. Although these skills are desirable in moderation (and great for the entrepreneur later), there is cause for alarm if the child shows a proclivity for getting away with something or regularly trying to get something for nothing.

Parents who are not straight with one another, either financially or emotionally, will have an effect on their kids. An effective tactic to counteract the hustler's schemes is to make sure that you, as parents, are in concert with one another regarding the decisions you make—then discuss those decisions with the child present. This is particularly important for divorced or divorcing parents.

The oblivious. A five- to eight-year-old may already be aware that in the world of Mom and Dad, money equals responsibility. If it doesn't look like much fun, the child will quite reasonably "check out" when the subject of money arises. "There's only trouble here," may be the inner fear of the oblivious child. Your money mentoring team may be of particular benefit to this child. If Mom and Dad communicate anxiety about money, members of the team may be able to present a calmer, more engaging relationship with the development of money skills.

And here's a gentle reminder to grown-ups who recognize some of their own habits in these styles: few of us got anything *like* the kind of intentional financial education we are suggesting for this next generation. If you were lucky, you had a parent or grandparent who gave you direction, some good advice, and some role modeling. Up until the 1980s, that was pretty much sufficient for about 80 percent of the population. Banks were highly regulated, many jobs came with pensions so if you hadn't been a saver there was still a safety net of some kind—and financial education was at best a quick reminder that compound interest is your friend. The economic world is vastly more complex today: deregulated, global, and volatile. If you feel you have not been an intentional money mentor for your kids up to this point, it's not a sign of bad parenting; it's an indication of how different the world is—and it's an opportunity to develop new skills in tandem with your children.

4. Family Money Values and Kids

Imagine you're a guest of the sometimes irritating, often provocative, cranky talk-show host Bill Maher, who asks a question about school prayer or military service. Whatever your views, your values probably would bubble to the surface in an instant. You know where you stand on these issues.

Now imagine being interviewed by NPR's financial journalist Kai Ryssdal, who asks, "What key values do you and your family hold that determine how you handle money?" Chances are, the answer might not be on the tip of your tongue with the same immediacy as your position on military service or the death penalty.

Some words and phrases may come to mind: *save for a rainy day, be responsible, don't spend more than you earn, share with the less fortunate, practice frugality, take risks, be generous with your kids.* The list, as we shall see in a minute, may be long. But few families have conversations—as a unit—that make the values clear and operative. Often, the expectation is that handling money wisely is common sense or something that comes with age (if only!).

To pinpoint your family values and whether you regularly put your money where your mouth is, consider these questions for yourself:

Some Financial Values Descriptors

Power

Independence

Status

Peace

Generosity

Quest for knowledge

Desire for family

Community-building

Social justice

Love

Conservation

- Do you feel an obligation to "give back"? Tally up the hours you volunteered last year, the pro bono work you did, or your total amount of contributions to charity. Do your actions match your beliefs?

- Do you subscribe to the notion that maintaining good health habits is basic to maintaining good health (and lowering health-care costs)? If you haven't worked out in months and your eating habits reflect high-cholesterol indulgence instead of a balanced diet, you may need to reassess your values.

- Is *carpe diem* the family slogan? If your retirement fund is empty, you may be living out your principles. But if some part of you holds that saving for a rainy day is a value you care about, then your actions may be out of sync with your aspirations.

- Do you think of yourself as a committed environmentalist but you don't recycle at home?

- Do you believe you and your kids must dress for success—even before you get there? You'll probably allot more to your clothing budget than your neighbors do—and you may be more tolerant of your kids' wants than if you believe a clothing budget should reflect the reality of your overall financial status.

Financial values go well beyond the basics of "saving for the future," "sharing with others," and "spending wisely." Financial values are intimately tied to your most basic actions, the way you spend your days, and the feelings you have about how you relate to the world. How you live your life is central to what you will teach your kids about money.

Money Values at Odds

It's one thing to talk about family values and quite another to talk about the financial values held by individual members of the family. Pretending that everyone is on the same page isn't enough.

Take a look at the Family Money Values chart for an illustration of how the differing values of each member of the family can set the stage for sending mixed messages to your kids.

Family Money Values		
	Mom	**Dad**
Earning	Having a lot of money isn't as important as being happy.	Being happy is earning a lot of money.
Spending		Spend on things that are high quality
Investing	Safe T-Bills and a good savings bank is where I want to invest our money.	It's foolish not to take some risk to make money grow more quickly.
Saving	We should be saving as a family.	Only one parent's income should go to savings.
Philanthropy	Five percent of total income should go to a good cause.	Two percent of my income goes to my college alumni fund.

Family Money Values

It isn't likely all family members are on the same page in terms of values, and if you're divorced, it may be even harder. (Though some of the best parenting I see is with parents who are divorced and determined to be consistent with their kids.) But in the interest of being good money mentors, it makes sense to reach some kind of financial détente. Ivan Lansberg, author of *Succeeding Generations: Realizing the Dream of Families in Business*, describes the notion of a "shared dream" or vision that effectively helps galvanize family energy and excitement in the shepherding and growth of family wealth. Setting financial expectations is a lot easier when kids and parents are in accord in terms of a family vision: where will the family be in twenty years? What are the family's aspirations and hopes? Once the family vision has been articulated, the next step is to establish some clear values

Daughter	Son	Aunt Em	Grandpa
Work? It interferes with my social life.	I want to work every weekend and after school.		
	It's my money— I can spend it any way I want.		Spend only on necessities. Luxuries are wasteful.
			Investing? I buy a lottery ticket every week; that's how I invest!
I can't afford to save now; I have expenses.		Enjoy life now; you won't live forever.	A wise man saves for the future.
	Why would anyone give money away?	My trust fund isn't large enough for me to give anything away.	Ten percent of my income goes to the church.

Family Money Values				
	Mom	Dad	Other	Other
Earning				
Spending				
Investing				
Saving				
Philanthropy				

that your kids can use as a financial lighthouse throughout their apprenticeship—and five- to eight-year-olds are not too young to benefit.

To help clarify your values, make copies of the blank Family Money Values chart. You and your spouse should first fill it in separately. Share it with any other family members who are central to the financial life of the family. Use the value words in the sidebar to help trigger thinking about your values. Then discuss the results.

Financial values become evident to kids through the stories they hear—from grandparents, parents, aunts, and uncles. Think of a story from your life about each of the money issues in the following chart and analyze it to determine what values you hold about that aspect of money.

Now ask other members of the family to do the same. When children are under ten, turn this into an oral storytelling session. As you share stories, conflicting and shared visions about money will emerge.

The Action	The Story	The Value Embodied in the Story
Earning		
Spending		
Saving and investing		
Philanthropy		

Getting family members aligned on their financial values will go a long way toward ending family dramas related to money as well as minimizing children's ability to exploit their parents' conflicting points of view! As a parent you have the authoritarian right to impose a decree: *we will have a set of values we live by as a family unit.* Here are some tactics to help you build consensus on values:

Create a family chart, website, collage, or graffiti poster—any tool for helping family members articulate in some visual way the family vision and money values that are relevant to a *family unit* (as distinct from individual needs or desires). Little kids, especially, love making wall-sized murals. Put up giant sheets of paper with the words *saving, spending,* and *sharing* written in big letters. Ask kids to draw an idea of what each word means. Then add the word *future* and have them do the same. The future is a pretty abstract concept for young ones. But having their mom or dad talk about the future is one way to give them a sense of what it actually means.

Don't try to take on too much. Identify one value at a time that everyone can rally round. For example, if giving back is an imperative that you hope your kids will adopt, make that a priority value to embody, model, reinforce, talk about, and act on. Or if taking time together as a family is a tradition you want to maintain, create a vacation savings pot and ask each family member to donate 1 percent of any money earned each month ($.03 if you make $2.50 stuffing envelopes for Mom this month; $50 if you make $5,000). The point is to find common goals and vehicles for making your family's life values operational.

There is no one-size-fits-all path to clarifying financial values. Every family has its own issues and needs. A single dad and his six-year-old daughter will have different challenges than a two-parent family with five kids, two incomes, and a significant trust fund. But both families may share the same fundamental values—and that's the key: working hard to get your financial values in sync will go a long way toward helping you raise a family whose members are conscious and careful about how they spend, earn, save, invest, and give money away.

5. Begin a Savings Program

Compound interest has been called the "eighth wonder of the world." And no wonder—even a modest savings plan, growing over the course of twenty years can reap results. As the effects of the Great Recession still linger, interest rates are currently well below 1 percent for many types of savings accounts. However, the point is *time*: over the next twenty or thirty years, interest rates will no doubt change. When it comes to savings, it is crucial to take the long view. Whether you have a sophisticated estate plan or are managing limited resources, creating a nest egg for your child emphasizes the importance of savings, and can be a crucial part of helping him achieve independence.

6. Calm Yourself; Calm Your Kids

Managing money makes a lot of people uneasy—but your job is to communicate to kids that managing money is as normal as brushing your teeth. In this first stage, kids will approach issues of money through the eyes of influential grown-ups. If you're anxious and uncomfortable yourself, you will communicate this to the kids. Here are suggestions for finding the calm that will make the financial apprenticeship a less stressful experience for all:

- Before taking kids shopping, spend some quiet time with them—a warm bath, a short walk, even a few minutes of quiet talk and hugging can lower the excitement level considerably.

- Stores—especially in a shopping mall environment—are intentionally and cleverly designed to overstimulate. This is to the store's advantage and your disadvantage. Too much time spent looking, wanting, being revved up by the lights, the sounds, the visual displays will exacerbate hyperactivity. Limit children's time and expectations while shopping. Decide what you are going to get before you go; set boundaries for time and money, and stick to both. This will give children clear messages and expectations about the experience.

- Help kids associate spending money with managing real needs, not filling empty places within the soul. Shopping to cheer kids up, reward good behavior, or entertain will establish patterns that will only be exacerbated as they grow older. There are far more emotionally satisfying ways to cheer kids up (chicken soup and an hour spent playing a game together are quite effective), reward good behavior (gold stars and a note from you saying how proud of them you are), and entertain them (read to or with them, build something together, go for a walk together).

For some people, yoga offers a vehicle for calm in the context of dealing with money. In an interview for *Yoga Journal*, Linda Wolff, who owns and operates a boutique in New York City, said, "I see people in my shop doing this neurotic shopping, spending way more than they can afford. I recognize them easily. There's a certain look in their eyes, a nervous energy, sort of a rush or a high. . . . I use to get that high myself, sometimes running up credit card bills of $30,000! I remember it used to feel great when I was buying. I'd feel free and alive—until I got the bill! It was like a disease. But my disease was cured by yoga. Something changed within. There came a calm, a balance, a feeling of being filled by myself and not by material stuff." You may not feel drawn to yoga as a way to calm yourself. But it's worth paying attention to any hyperactivity that emerges for you and your kids in relation to financial matters and worth working to soothe counterproductive feelings. Meditation, exercise, or a simple cup of tea are all good ways to soothe money monsters.

Moving On

Stage One, "I'm just a kid," is a time to have fun with and enjoy the five- to eight-year-olds in your life. They are curious, always exploring and discovering. When you can introduce them to something new that helps them master their growing world—while having a great time with you—you are launching great kids.

Money Messages

Think of these as financial fortune cookie–style messages.

Keep them simple and stick them into book bags and pockets, under pillows . . .

I love you more than all the money in the world.

Saving money is as important as brushing your teeth!

Being stingy is mean, but giving money away too easily is silly! Love, Dad

A nickel is the same as how many pennies? A gold star for the right answer!

Find and save twenty nickels, and I'll give you a crisp new dollar bill and a quarter! Love, Mom

Saving, sharing, and spending money wisely will keep you financially safe.

Only borrow what you know you can pay back.

Time is money. Use it well.

"Great is the human who has not lost his childlike heart."

MENCIUS (MENG-TSE), 400 BCE

Stage Two
Ages 9–12: Encouraging Passions

Remember when you were ten or twelve and suddenly everything mattered deeply to you? It may have been when you first read *The Diary of Anne Frank* or *Black Beauty*. Or perhaps it was when you first saw *Old Yeller*.

Those feelings, so tender and strong, help us, as children, move from a focus on self to a focus on others. We identify with characters in books, movies, and cartoons, and we begin to have empathy for and interest in a world that is both reflective of and larger than ourselves. This is a time when best friends become all-important, when passions for hobbies or animals or causes first emerge. That awakening to the larger world brings with it a panoply of feelings, a sense that things really matter. Children now enter Stage Two of the financial apprenticeship. Remembering these qualities as you choose money activities and resources from the following chart will help you make meaningful connections for the child who is morphing from a little kid to a "tween," perched on the edge of a new independence.

The Life/Money Map Stage Two/Ages 9–12	
Social/Emotional Development	**Appropriate Money Skills to Master**
Is growing fast, body changing	Can make change
Feels self-conscious	Shows initiating behavior and entrepreneurial spirit
Begins to exhibit self-expression and independence	Shows awareness of the cost of things
Begins to develop social conscience	Shows awareness of earned money
Becomes aware of hobbies and careers	Can balance a simple checking account and keep up with a savings account
Identifies with peer groups	

Flip Open

3. How to spend wisely	4. How to talk about money	5. How to live on a budget	6. How to invest
Organize a Mall Scavenger Hunt (see page 30).	Invite your child to write a short play about loaning money to a friend who doesn't give it back on time. Offer to read the parts with him.	Deposit allowance straight into a checking account and make sure there are one or two items that can be paid by check. Hold her accountable for a balanced checkbook before the next deposit.	Order annual reports from your kid's favorite compa[n] (Timberland, Netflix, Stonybrook Yogurt) and as[k] him to find out the name o[f] the president of the comp[any,] how much money the com[-]pany made in the previous[s] year, and how much mone[y] spent on marketing.
Demonstrate how to read unit labels on a product that matters to your child (pet food, potato chips, juice)—is it cheaper to purchase an individual package, a multipack, or by the pound?	Make time to talk about a family money vision.	Designate a favorite activity and keep the receipts for a month. Have kids tally the receipts and consider what they might otherwise do with that money.	Ask your child to try to stu[mp] you with money words tak[en] from the financial section [of] the newspaper. Offer him [a] quarter for every word you get wrong. Or give him a list of words to look up, an[d] a quarter for each one he memorizes.
Discuss the difference between needs, wants, and wishes.	Have kids track the family electric bill for six months as a way to talk about energy, alternative energy, and saving energy. Or track the cost of gas for a few months. What does it cost to travel to and from a favorite destination?	Give your child a budget for a weekend family dinner. Let her create the menu and do the shopping (accompany her or send her with a money mentor).	Encourage children to coll[ect] things that gain value ove[r] time (stamps, fossils, com[ic] books).
Alert kids to the danger of accumulating interest on purchases. Charge interest on any small loans you make so she understands the concept in a concrete way.		Have kids track you with a camera, taking a photo of every way you spend money. At the end of the day, the photos will tell a story about what you care about.	
Teach kids to compare prices at different stores to find the best deal. Comparison shopping is conscious shopping.	Spelling bees can be fun; now try *numbers* bees on a long car ride. Kids who can recall multiplication and division tables—without a calculator—will have a greater capacity to manage a budget or a business plan.	Give your kid a take-out menu and a dollar amount and ask her to order dinner for the family.	
Offer financial self-defense by pointing to hidden messages in ads. What are they promising? Do they really deliver?			
FTC's online game Ad Mongo is a fun lesson in decoding ads. http://bit.ly/AdMongo	BizWords, available through the online store at www.independentmeans.com	*Math Doesn't Suck: How to Survive Middle School Math*, Danica McKellar	*When I Grow Up I'm Going to Be a Millionaire (A Children's Guide to Mutu[al] Funds)*, Ted Lea and Lora
PBS's Don't Buy It site is dated but still great consumer education (pbskids.org/dontbuyit)	*It Pays to Talk: How to Have the Essential Conversations with Your Family About Money and Investing*, Carrie Schwab-Pomerantz and Charles Schwab	*Neale S. Godfrey's Ultimate Kids' Money Book*, Neale S. Godfrey	An online broker for long-term investors: www.sharebuilder.com
PBS's Loop Scoop series of cartoons introduces the environmental consequences of our purchases (pbskids.org/loopscoops)	*Blunders* is a manners-learning board game. www.blundersmania.com	*Hometown Money: How to Enrich Your Community with Local Currency*, Paul Glover	*Growing Money: A Comple[te] Investing Guide for Kids*, Gail Karlitz
		www.madisonhours.org	www.lavamind.com
		www.quicken.com	
		www.kidsbank.com	

w to exercise the preneurial spirit	8. How to handle credit	9. How to use money to change the world	10. How to be a citizen of the world
your child a story t an entrepreneur who d a passion into a ness.	Create a mock credit card that can be used for purchases against your kid's allowance.	Have a family meeting on a charity gift that matters to the whole family.	On Sunday nights, challenge kids to answer trivia from the weekend news, offering a reasonable incentive for getting the correct answer.
v an Entrepreneur's day Party. Use the uct-in-a-Box Activity r the main event.	Offer to loan money for a special request, and write a contract you and your child both have to sign. Charge interest if	Ask your child to arrange a Goodwill or Salvation Army pick-up of family castaways and have her estimate the value for tax purposes.	Invite their friends for an international movie night with international cuisine (pizza does not
te an Entrepreneur's f Fame. Pay your child rter for each picture or she collects about an preneur she discovers. a gallery in her room e pictures.	he exceeds his allotted time to pay you back. Talk about the privileges they want (later bedtimes, more play dates) and how they	Show kids a tax return. Explain what *tax-deductible* means. Many kids are unaware of how social service networks provide assistance. Talk	count). Learn the words and meaning of at least one song sung in another language.
preneurs see solutions e others see just prob- . When kids start to e, offer to pay them for ution to whatever they omplaining about.	can demonstrate they're ready for them by earn- ing your trust. Agree to an allowance advance as a way	about service projects affili- ated with your congregation or their school. Host a forum for sharing (or developing) family mission	
time you hear an idea one of your kids, jump Offer to help create a to bring it to life.	to demonstrate the mechanics of credit. Insist on a payment plan including due dates, interest, and late fees.	statements. Let kids listen in (and add their two cents to) your giving decisions. Help kids brainstorm how to solve a problem.	
uct-in-a-Box Activity vailable through www pendentmeans.com *Toothpaste Millionaire*, Merrill	*From Seashells to Credit Cards: Money and Currency* by Ernestine Giesecke *The Black Stallion* by Walter Farley	The Giraffe Heroes Project is a group that encourages kids to stick their necks out for the common good: Giraffe.org *Marching for Freedom: Walk Together, Children, and Don't You Grow Weary*, Elizabeth Partridge 21/64 Picture Your Legacy Cards Kids Care Clubs: www.kidscare.org *The Giving Family: Raising Our Children to Help Others*, Susan Crites Price http://encyclopediaofgratitude .tumblr.com	Three of our favorite kid-approved interna- tional movies: *Ponyo*, *The Secret of Kells*, *Bend It Like Beckham* www.globegenie.com

Parents need to talk with

their kids about money as comfortably

as they discuss the weather.

The Ten Basic Money Skills

This chart will help you reinforce the big tasks of this period.

		Basic Money Skill	
		1. How to save	**2. How to get paid what you're worth**
Actions: 9–12 Years		Help children save for a special interest, event, or goal. Make a regular deposit that cannot be disturbed until the end of the year and is used expressly for the stated purpose of achieving a dream or goal. Offer a non-monetary bonus if she meets her goals (such as toys, tickets to a sports event with you). If interest rates under half a percent are too insubstantial to get your ten-year-old interested, supplement this return with your own interest payment—say, 4 percent every month or quarter. At this stage, it may be easier to hear you in a note than to absorb what may sound like a lecture. Once a month, put a money message related to saving under her pillow. A text would work well, too! (See page 90 for suggestions.)	Encourage kids to research the going rate for babysitting, lawn mowing, and other chores by interviewing friends or going online. Role-play the part of a prospective client who asks, "What do you charge?" Let your child practice his response. (This is a good task to ask a money mentor team member to do.) Send your kids on a quest to www.monster.com for information on how much a teacher, a lawyer, an astronaut, an actress, a bioengineer, and a waitperson make. Talk about why there are differences in salaries. Challenge kids to take on a "grown-up" task (wash the dog, make dessert, paint a bookshelf or other used furniture). Pay for the extra effort.
Resources		*The Everything Kids' Money Book: Earn It, Save It, and Watch It Grow*, Brette McWorter Sember *The First National Bank of Dad: The Best Way to Teach Kids About Money*, David Owen www.orangekids.com	*The Babysitter's Handbook: The Care and Keeping of Kids*, Harriet Brown

The difference between

a fantasy and the realization of a dream

is having the financial skills

to make the fantasy come to life.

Big Tasks for Stage Two

There can be giant differences in maturation levels between nine- and twelve-year-olds. The nine-year-old may still want to retreat to a tree house or her bedroom or to the park with friends, whereas the twelve-year-old may long for more distant destinations and more complex activities. But their emerging passions and growing awareness of the world around them are similar, so if you have children in this age range, you'll want to attend to the following big tasks:

1. Provide Ten Basic Money Skills activities to leverage each child's passions and quest for independence at a higher level of challenge.

2. Help them make independent decisions in the face of fierce peer pressure. Establishing clear boundaries gives kids support to act on established principles and values—in life, as well as in financial dealings. Boundaries provide both a guide and a backup system for an emerging moral compass. This may be a challenge with tenacious children, intent on doing what "everyone else" is doing. But you're the grown-up—without your courage and strength, children have nothing but their own unformed judgment and the pressure of the external culture to guide their development at this stage.

3. Make connections between developing passions and interests and funding those passions. The image of the starving artist or struggling writer may be romantic, but penury isn't a necessary ingredient for a creative life. Whether kids are showing interest in the arts, helping the homeless, or the ubiquitous lemonade stand, now is the time to introduce the concept of sustainability. Helping them make financial plans for *whatever* they wish to do is a good way to give them tools to turn dreams to action.

4. Reinforce the rule that behavior has financial consequences. Making this connection helps kids develop a solid foundation for the next three phases of their financial apprenticeship.

5. Introduce role models. One way to help young people see how to turn their dreams into real-life possibilities is to give them access to people (including yourself) who have pursued their passions into careers, achievements, and avocations.

I. Ten Basic Money Skills: Encouraging Passion

The Life/Money Map for the nine- to twelve-year-old assumes a greater level of self-reliance and self-expression than existed earlier and takes into account the energy and power of young passions. Those passions are vehicles for encouraging financial curiosity and responsibility within a context that matters to children. For example, if your ten-year-old declares she's a vegetarian, you can ask her to help you shop for food suitable to her life choice, giving her a budget that is comparable to the one for what the rest of the family eats (and if you are all vegetarians, so much the better—food budgets are great teaching tools). Or if your eleven-year-old son is well into collecting NBA trading cards, now is the time to teach him that saving and preserving those cards may be a kind of saving or investment strategy. If you have a collection of your own to pull out or can demonstrate what the 1956 Mickey Mantle first edition is worth today (and what you originally paid for it), you'll be a hit.

And this is the time to introduce the idea of entry-level jobs and salaries as practice for mastery of skills and knowledge. In 2000, a survey done by Junior Achievement indicated that 24 percent of teens believed they would be millionaires by the time they were thirty. And in September 2011, according to an AP/CNBC Poll, 20 percent of Americans said they'll be millionaires in the next decade, compared with 8 percent of United Kingdom residents. But only one in every twenty households was a millionaire in 2010, the AP reported, and more than 60 percent of Americans say it's "very unlikely" that they'll be worth $1 million by 2020.

Fueled by the get-rich-quick mentality of the Internet and the seeming overnight success of athletes and celebrities, kids begin to feel entitled to wealth at a precocious stage. Introducing nine- to twelve-year-olds to the reality that entry-level NBA players are paid an average of $74,000 per year (still not bad) rather than astronomical LeBron-sized salaries or that a beginning doctor makes considerably less than an experienced surgeon—and that everyone pays taxes—helps establish realistic expectations early.

Many of the activities related to this stage are iterations of tasks you may have done or resources shared with children when they were younger. What's different now is *who they are*. Their growing ability to question and analyze means that their conversations with you will be more complex and interesting.

Milly and Lily are two twelve-year-olds who, just few years ago, were oblivious to the costs of the infrastructure of their lives. That they had a phone to use, transportation, food, and shelter was simply a fact of life, nothing to be considered a big deal. But on a field trip with a money mentor, the two girls were asked to create a "lifestyle budget." They made choices about what they wanted in their lives: the kind of car they could imagine driving, how much time they would spend talking on the phone, what their monthly clothes budget would be, how much they would eat, and where they wanted to live.

At twelve, they now had context. Both girls went clothes shopping with their parents and understood the costs of fashion. Milly had a fifteen-minute-a-night phone budget. They understood that when their parents stopped for gas, someone had to pay for it. As the girls made lifestyle choices, their mentor helped them tally up an estimated cost of each of their choices. Each girl made a set of choices that came to about $35,000 per year in costs. Then they fantasized about the kind of jobs they wanted. One had dreams of being a photographer and artist; the other wanted to be a teacher. They were selecting from life choices that seemed exciting and real.

But as they learned about actual entry-level salaries for teachers in private schools (Milly's choice) and the time it takes to "make it big" as a photographer or artist (Lily's choice), both girls began to grasp that they had to make the two visions—lifestyle and career—work in concert. At twelve, they could now grasp that their dreams had a price tag they had to plan for.

This is the fertile ground of Stage Two. Kids needn't be discouraged by reality at this juncture, but they do need the right tools to deal with it.

This is also the time to begin encouraging Oprah-sized dreams—as she so eloquently puts it, "I dream so big it hurts my eyes"—instilling the idea that anything is possible. Too often, in spite of idolizing star athletes and video game creators on the one hand, children's dreams are pinched and small because grown-ups pooh-pooh their grandiose visions or treat them condescendingly. If children's dreams push up against the reality of what may be required to attain them, adults have a responsibility to guide them along their path with useful information and resources—not to squelch those dreams. Steve Jobs's father introduced him to engineers who took him seriously as a boy; and, say what you will about Tiger Mom, she encouraged her girls to think big from a very young age. Big is not necessarily better, but kids who are not encouraged to think they can take on the impossible will, by default, think small.

Skills for Passionate Lives

The difference between a fantasy and the realization of a dream is having the skills and financial acumen to make the fantasy come to life. By giving kids instruction in the language of money and business, as well as a vote of confidence that they are building the capacity to make their dreams come true, you tell them, "I take you seriously. I respect you and support your dreams."

Of course, it is also your job to instill responsibility and help them stay grounded. Parents who push kids to start businesses or reach for celebrity at a very early age may be pursuing their own unfulfilled dreams, and not those of their children. But there is no harm in helping kids think about what it takes to make a dream come true. The Ten Basic Money Skills activities will help you stick to reality while encouraging young passions.

Stage Two is sometimes characterized by family drama: tantrums about wants and wishes, anxieties about being different from or similar to peers, struggles around power and control. Sometimes these big tensions can seem unbearable to both kids and parents. But, at least where money is involved, kids who are clear about values and expectations will spend less time playing out big dramatic scenes than those who are trying to outfox you because the rules are not clear. And if you continue to create a calming environment in the financial spheres of your children's lives, you will mitigate those hormone-injected dramas.

2. Dealing with Peer Pressure and Money Decisions

This is the stage when, for kids, the stakes seem huge. To be in or out of the popular crowd matters. To be unique but just like everyone else is the impossible quest, and to be "cool" is imperative. It is at this point that parents become a critical counterbalance to the power of peers. Just because your daughter *says* everyone is buying Prada jackets doesn't make it essential for her to have one. And just because that new motorized bike is appearing in every driveway doesn't mean you need to rush out and add one to all the toys already taking up room in your garage.

In spite of the rolled eyes and the world-weary "Whatever," many kids would be perfectly happy to be out of the preadolescent rat race if their parents would just take them off the hook. If a kid can say to his friends, "My dad is a jerk and won't allow [fill in the blank]," you get to be the bad guy, and he can still seem cool. Parents who let their kids run the show, abdicating their prerogative as grown-ups, give kids no place to hide from their peers.

How to Handle Peer Pressure

The following real-life scenarios offer ways to help kids use financial values to deal with peer pressure—and their own emerging passions.

Scenario 1: The sleepovers and play dates that eleven-year-old Samantha and her friends had enjoyed since they were five or six evolved into weekly treks to the mall to see movies. Parents took turns dropping off and picking up the girls. Over time, the movie date began to include an extra hour, then two, to hang out at the mall. But this required extra money for food and the shopping that seemed an inevitable part of the mall experience.

Samantha's parents were increasingly uncomfortable with the amount of money she asked for every week, but they felt it was important for Samantha to be part of her girl group and didn't want to make her feel like an outsider. Though Samantha's parents could afford the outings, they were concerned their daughter was spending too much time "consuming" and not enough time developing herself in other ways. *What could they do?*

Scenario 2: Twins Ray and Rex played for the same Little League team in their community. The twins' parents had five children and struggled to keep up with the need for new equipment and uniforms for the boys, who seemed to grow faster as spring turned into summer. The little boys loved the game, and being part of a team was helping them develop individual personalities. Their parents struggled with the tension of wanting to encourage their sons' team activities while juggling the family budget. *What could they do?*

Scenario 3: Twelve-year-old Ashley seemed mature beyond her years, and many of her girlfriends were a couple of years older. When Ashley began to press for money to buy clothes that looked more like those of her older friends and were inappropriate for her age, her parents faced the challenge of how to rein in their daughter's sartorial tastes without making her give up her friends, too. *What could they do?*

Scenario 4: Nine-year-old Roxie lived with her dad, a widower, and his new wife. Roxie's loving dad had been indulgent after Roxie's mother died, and the little girl had lived in a state of financial anarchy since she was five. Whatever her friends did, Roxie wanted to do too—and Dad never said no. Roxie's stepmom was troubled by the habits she saw Roxie developing—spoiled and demanding—but father and daughter resisted attempts to alter the patterns they had developed between them. Dad was convinced Roxie needed be "part of the club" and refused to set limits on anything she wanted to do with the "club." *What could the stepmom do?*

What would you do in these cases? How could clarity about family values and money have helped these kids and their parents? When we put these cases to a panel of experienced parents, here are some suggestions they offered.

Scenario 1 Solution: The weekly movie is nearly as much a break for the parents as for the girls (having a tween occupied so you can get your own errands done is, after all, a great relief), so we don't want to disparage this activity too quickly. However, letting kids turn into mall rats as a form of babysitting suggests a lack of imagination. A conversation among the parents of four or five girls could easily produce a schedule in which parents take turns once a month offering alternative activities. (This is a particularly good alternative for girls who find Girl Scouts no longer cool enough but who would still benefit from the structure and direction such an organization offers.) Cutting out the movie-and-mall trip altogether isn't necessary, but cutting it back from once a week to once a month can make it a special activity once again.

One parent might take the girls to a flea market or on a tour of garage sales to hunt down quirky and inexpensive bargains— tracking down great vintage clothing, for example, can be both fun and financially enlightening. Another parent can offer an afternoon of games or a video festival at home (popcorn and movie magazines for all). One parent could lead a hike or organize an afternoon volunteering at the local Humane Society; yet another might provide cooking lessons, help the kids start their first investment club or charity circle, or get them started with a new hobby, such as collecting stamps or creating photo journals to document their outings together. The idea is to give the kids ways to bond that do not make consumerism recreation.

As kids get older and increasingly independent, parent-led activities get harder to organize. But this is another opening for the nonparent money mentor. The girls might not be enthusiastic about an afternoon with Molly's mom, but the same activity with Janet's hip Aunt Susan could be pretty appealing. And expanding the girls' vision of how to spend their free time will have positive effects on the choices they make for themselves in the next stage of their apprenticeship.

Scenario 2 Solution: When growth in family income doesn't keep pace with how fast children grow, parents may be hard-pressed to provide the props and equipment required for team sports, whether it's cheerleading or football, soccer or lacrosse. And twins double the challenge. But parents can build a community to help manage the pressures of a peer-driven world in which having all the requisite "stuff" feels so crucial to kids.

In this case, the twins' parents can work with other parents to create a uniform and equipment "recycling" program. This has the dual effect of bringing down the cost of team participation for everyone while sending messages about sharing and conservation. Such a program takes the stigma off so-called "poor kids," while underscoring the message for everyone that recycling is good for both the environment and family finances. Children are highly sensitive about class issues or being seen as "needy" and may drop out of sports rather than take part in a program that requires expenses beyond their parents' means. It takes some lobbying and organizing to get all parents to participate, but phone calls to parent leaders and plans to set up the recycling center near the kids' playing grounds, will make this resource the first stop—rather than a last resort—for parents and kids. Opting for the financial smart choice in this case is also the green choice.

Scenario 3 Solution: Ashley's dilemma is a common one for girls who are growing up fast and find themselves developing—physically and socially—more quickly than some of their peers. Forcing girls to hang out with younger friends "just because" isn't very useful. Development has a life of its own—your best hope is to support it with wisdom rather than fight it. On the other hand, there's no point in helping your daughter or son mature more quickly than is necessary—he or she may *look* and *feel* older and wiser, but do you really want your twelve-year-old driving in cars with sixteen- and seventeen-year-olds?

Ashley wants to express herself as a more mature young woman and thinks of clothes as a way to do that. Give her another option. This is the time to revisit the allowance and discuss how handling her money is a more enduring form of exhibiting maturity. Offer to increase the allowance to cover all clothing purchases. Suggest a trial period of three or six months to give her a chance to make a few mistakes and get on track again. (We all make buying mistakes—one bad choice is probably not enough to kill the experiment, but a pattern of belly-exhibiting shirt purchases but no socks may be enough to justify a modification of the rules.) If, all along, the allowance has been treated as a teaching tool, not a salary or entitlement, Ashley will be able to demonstrate that she is gaining wisdom with her maturity. If not, the clothing allowance will be reduced until she's ready for another try.

The key here is respecting the child's struggle to grow and mature, providing tools with which she can demonstrate to you and to herself—not to mention her friends—that she is in fact older and more "in charge." Indeed, if her older friends still can't balance a checkbook and are financially clueless, she may soon feel more grown-up than they are! The more confident she feels about her skills, the easier it will be to be her own person. Spa owner and former professional skater Sheila Cluff recalls that when she was sixteen and on tour with the Ice Capades she made money loaning money—with interest—to older girls who were far less money savvy than she was!

Scenario 4 Solution: In this case, the problem is less about peers and more about Roxie's father's reliance on her friends for signals about how to make her happy. Perhaps the best her stepmom can offer—(her position being much like that of an aunt or a close family friend)—is another model of reality. Although intervening in the established father-daughter dynamic may be neither feasible nor effective, the stepmom can at least make sure she doesn't join the anarchy and exacerbate the problem. By keeping clear the expectations she has of Roxie when they are together, over time both father and daughter may be able to let go of some of their old patterns. If not, eventually either the father will have to deal with the problem or Roxie will have to experience the consequences—it's not the responsibility of the stepmom. But if the stepmom and father can establish a shared financial vision, it is likely that the new family system will share the benefits.

3. Making the Connection: The Cost of Passion

A child with a phenomenal voice can capitalize on that talent by working hard, studying with the best teachers, and devoting time and energy to the pursuit of his passion for music. Or he can hope he will overcome the odds, be selected for any of the myriad *Star Search* or *American Idol* TV competitions, and win the brass ring. If you don't have the good fortune to have the lottery-winning child in your household, a good backup plan is to encourage his passions in a reality-based fashion that preserves the wild enthusiasm required to triumph over the typical challenges to dearly held visions.

Anyone who has raised a prodigy or even a moderately talented child knows that financial obligations often go hand in hand with supporting the child's gifts. Frequently I hear parents talk proudly about children who are athletically, musically, or intellectually gifted in one form or another—then they follow the praise with a vow that they will "do everything possible" to help those children realize their potential (the quest for Olympic gold these days can easily run into hundreds of thousands of dollars and more). Rarely does that involve helping their kids be conscious and purposeful about how to meet the financial obligations of funding their heart's desires.

Thus we have children who strain or drain family resources while they feed their talent and, worse, young people who hit the proverbial financial wall when they run out of funds for training or experiences that might well have provided the boost they needed to get to the top. Teaching kids to think about how to fund their passions prepares them for the high-stakes pursuit of big dreams as they mature—and emboldens them to go after even bigger dreams. This requires that parents share economic truths and help kids confront real challenges. Here are stories of three families who have done just that.

Graciela, *a young skater, was one of five children. She had been skating since she was six, and at eleven she had become interested in the competitive side of the sport. Although it didn't seem she was on a track to the Olympics, Graciela was good enough to compete in regional and state events. This called for private coaching, skating costumes, long-distance driving to events, accommodation expenses, and myriad other details that accompany the world of kids and ice.*

Although financially comfortable, the family worried that funding Graciela's passion to skate competitively might divert resources from the dreams of their other children. Prepared to make sacrifices, they wanted to make sure their daughter was sufficiently committed to stay the course—and responsible enough to take part in the demands of the sport. They agreed to help her fund her dream, but on the condition that she be involved in budgeting and decision making related to becoming a competitive skater.

The first year, Graciela's parents worked with her to draw up a list of all the annual costs of competing. They required two things of Graciela: that she make sure all expenses for her sport were recorded in a journal and documented with receipts and that she take on an extra family chore to acknowledge the cost of her skating. She chose to be in charge of caring for the family's houseplants and weeding her mother's flower and vegetable gardens in the summer, and it was also her job to clean out and wipe down the family refrigerator once a month. None of the extra chores was inherently difficult, but as she carried them out, she connected her desire to skate with the effort it took to make her desire possible.

Though Graciela won a number of competitions, by the time she was seventeen she'd come to terms with the fact she was not of Olympic caliber. However, she still loved to skate and knew it would be part of her life somehow in an ongoing way. And with each year she skated, she had taken on more and more of the financial responsibility for her activity, no doubt getting a head start on her decision to start a company when she was twenty-seven. Handling money was second nature to her by then.

Ten-year-old Tyrone had been playing the piano since he was four. He could read music with ease and was composing by the time he was seven. Tyrone's parents lived in a school district that offered excellent music instruction, and his teacher had, for a modest fee, been giving him private lessons on weekends.

When the local school district, in a round of cost cutting, eliminated the music program, Tyrone's parents were devastated. They were unable to afford additional private lessons of the caliber he needed and could not see how they were going to support his gift. At their wits' end, Tyrone's parents respected their son enough to discuss the terrible dilemma with him. Heartbroken, they announced that he would have to take time off from his lessons until they could save money to hire a new tutor or find another public school with an advanced music program.

But Tyrone was a step ahead of them. The precocious boy mentioned he had met a few people who had come to hear him play at the school and thought that perhaps one of them would give him lessons if he had something to barter. The parents were not enthusiastic about putting a ten-year-old out to earn music lessons, but the idea sparked them to explore options in the community. Eventually they struck a deal with the music director of a community church. In exchange for Mom working four hours a week in the church soup kitchen, Tyrone could have lessons with the church music director.

Eventually the family got their son enrolled in another school with a good music program, and the young boy continued his studies. This is not a fairy tale in which the young prodigy finds a fairy godmother who sends him off to Juilliard and he goes on to win the Van Cliburn competition. It's a story of a family who, rather than hide a difficult reality from their child, engaged him and gave him a chance to be part of the solution.

Children who feel helpless and hopeless because information is withheld from them will grow up with the long-term consequences of being left out of problem-solving opportunities. It is sometimes lack of information that makes kids turn away from financial responsibility—if something seems mysterious and outside their ken, they may sense danger and put the blinders on. If you want kids to be responsible for pursuing their own passions, you have to include them in real-life discussions and decisions.

Stretching Visions

Connecting financial responsibility with the pursuit of passion is part of the work of Stage Two; expanding their vision is another. These are the years when the first entrepreneurial urges may show up. The budding desire to have a business may present itself as a form of play (I'll play the boss . . .), and parents would do well to take such ideas seriously, encouraging enterprising behavior. This is curiosity at work. Channel it.

If your ten-year-old wants to set up a lemonade stand (or a more contemporary venture—say, carrot juice or healthy muffins), go along with the activity, but make sure she adds up the cost of the ingredients to determine how much to charge for each item. And if she initially wants to set up shop outside the house on a street with no foot traffic, help her find a location where she'll actually get some business (maybe an aunt or a good friend lives in a more fruitful location).

Try connecting a child's enterprise to something bigger than herself: What will she do with the profits? How will this idea make the community a better place? How might the business make a difference to friends and family? Can she imagine being responsible for more than one lemonade stand around town?

Condescending to children ("Isn't that cute, honey" or "You have no idea what you're doing" or "Don't be silly") squanders the teachable moment. You don't want to badger kids with an obsessive attention to money at every turn, but you do want to acknowledge that your little girl or boy is beginning to think, act, choose, and see herself or himself in new ways. Supporting that growth gives kids a leg up in the next stage of development.

Occasionally families tell me, "My child really doesn't have to work. He has a healthy trust fund and is set for life. Why should I encourage money-making activities if they aren't necessary?" And of course the response to that question lies in each family's vision of what you want for your kids. But work is not just about the money. What kind of child do you want to raise? What purpose do you hope your child might aspire to, and how will you prepare him or her to achieve that purpose? Children at *all* income levels who master work experiences tend to have greater self-confidence and self-worth than those whose primary activity has been to satisfy themselves or to consume.

Even kids who have the opportunity to delve deeply into studies or pursuits that may not be financially fruitful (life as a painter or poet, for example) find they feel better about themselves if they know they possess the savvy to be financially independent.

Connecting work with earning money is valuable in developing responsible work habits, acquiring discipline, and understanding the need to make hard choices. Who doesn't have a positive image of the Girl Scout who sells more cookies than anyone (and who actually sells them herself, rather than having her parents sell for her at the office) or the newspaper delivery kid who shows up reliably every morning? These children are developing work habits that tangibly demonstrate the connection between labor and reward, drive and fulfilling passions. Over three decades of working with kids has provided plenty of evidence that those who start early have an easier time mastering those skills than kids who aren't required to work for pay until after high school or even college.

> Connecting work with earning money is valuable in developing responsible work habits, acquiring discipline, and understanding the need to make hard choices.

So how can Stage Two kids earn money? With so many parts of the economy professionalized or automated, even the old standbys like delivering papers, mowing lawns, and washing cars are vanishing as early learning experiences. Here are suggestions from families who are solving that dilemma.

Make kids "subcontractors" for your work projects. Is there something you can delegate? Stuffing envelopes? Paying by the number of envelopes stuffed gives a tangible sense of value. Entering addresses into your contact file? Fifteen cents for every address will do it for the 10-year-old; 12-year-olds demand a little more. (Some kids will handle this task more quickly and easily than you can.)

**Good Moneymaking
Chores for Kids**

Polishing Dad's shoes

Washing Mom's car

Watering plants for a
neighbor

Reshelving books

Walking the neighbor's
dog

Organizing the tool closet

Addressing party
invitations

Performing computer
maintenance (e.g.,
cleaning the keyboard)

Hire kids for personal projects. Cleaning up their rooms should be a normal part of their own responsibility; however, refolding all of *your* sweaters and putting them away, cleaning up those drawers into which you throw odds and ends, polishing your shoes, or reshelving the books you have left out deserves compensation. Other extras might include helping to plant seedlings in the spring, putting away lawn furniture in the fall, or helping a relative or friend with chores. Work you would hire out to a third party is appropriate to offer kids—as long as it's safe, of course.

Keep a running list of "projects for cash" posted in the kitchen. Whenever your kids plead boredom, have them select a project and earn some money for their saving, spending, and giving jars.

The respect that comes from work performed outside the home is satisfying for kids. Walking the dog or feeding the fish and guinea pigs at home is part of family duties; walking or washing the neighbor's pets is an opportunity to earn extra income. Encourage kids to create flyers to post in the neighborhood for whatever service they're interested in offering, and brainstorm other—safe—ways to notify friends, family, and neighbors of their services. At this stage they are still a little young to be heavily involved in social media.

As your kids' entrepreneurial instincts kick in, help them turn ideas into money. Is the garage or attic in need of a serious purge? If your kids help out, share the proceeds of a garage sale with them. Make sure the help is real (helping to select what will be sold, marking prices on items for sale, setting up tables, making posters and flyers to advertise, being present at the sale to help with customers and make change). At the conclusion of the sale, calculate the profits with them by deducting any costs that are appropriate. These are the early—and totally natural—ways that kids first begin to understand profits, margins, expenses, and so on.

When a child shows interest in starting a business, help her create a business plan. Whether it's a proposal to run birthday parties for younger kids or selling the fishing flies she makes, by walking her through the basics of target markets, product or service costs, pricing, and how to market her goods you will get her thinking about the questions and puzzles she needs to solve to make money.

One of my favorite stories is of eleven-year-old Corey, who was for some years my next-door neighbor. The local softball teams played in a field near our neighborhood and drew a crowd every weekend, but there was no hot dog stand or anyone selling soft drinks to the spectators. Corey saw a moneymaking opportunity and talked his mother into taking him to a discount store where he bought cases of soft drinks. The next weekend he bought ice, piled it into a red wagon left over from his "childhood," and hauled the wagon to the game. He sold out his stock in an hour. Corey quickly became a fixture at the games, providing a much-needed service—and gaining real lessons about business.

> **Suggested Nominees for the Entrepreneur's Gallery**
>
> Mark Zuckerberg, Facebook
>
> Chad Hurley, YouTube
>
> Richard Branson, Virgin Atlantic
>
> Lady Gaga, Music and Philanthropy
>
> Steve Jobs, Apple Computer
>
> Sara Blakely, Spanks
>
> Roxanne Quimby, Burt's Bees

As he grew more confident, Corey decided to branch out. Because it was summer, he had weekdays off between games, so he decided to take his wagon closer to town and sell soda to tourists who came to visit during the summer. Again, his business did well: out-of-towners were charmed to buy from a young boy selling soda out of a red wagon, and because he was a sociable child, they also learned a little about the town. (Note: this is a small town and Corey was never out of sight of people who were keeping an eye on him. Enterprise for kids should never trump safety.)

Cody learned a lot that summer—not just about business, but also the politics of commerce. One of the local merchants, resenting the "competition," called city officials and complained the boy was operating without a license.

Suddenly the eleven-year-old was thrust into battle with the bureaucracy. Undaunted, Corey talked his mom into helping him apply for—and win—a street vender's license. The next summer he was back in business. Imagine learning at eleven what it takes some people another twenty years to do!

4. Behavior Has Financial Consequences

The years from nine to twelve are prime time for helping kids learn to make choices—sometimes hard choices—that have consequences. Delayed gratification is still challenging at this stage, and you may have to endure the acting out that comes from primal frustration, but keep in mind that you're the grown-up and dealing with this is part of your job.

Bruce Cameron is a great model for teaching children about financial consequences. When his children were young, Cameron, creator of a very funny syndicated column on which the now-defunct sitcom *8 Simple Rules for Dating My Teenage Daughter* was based, wrote a piece for *Time* magazine describing what was then considered a radical approach to financial awareness. To get his kids' attention, he printed out a Quicken account of the family finances, showing every penny of income and "out go" for the family, sparing no detail. (He did take some time to explain to his children the nature of the trust he was bestowing on them with this information—and his expectation that they would not betray that trust by blabbing the information to their friends.) He described the experience this way:

At first my children were shocked to see how much money I made—wow, we were rich! But then I showed them how much money the government took off the top, how much we spent, and how little was left at the end of the month. When they saw our credit-card balances, they actually got angry: Why hadn't I done something about this earlier? The results of the family meeting were immediate. My children had always rolled their eyes when I suggested that not every single light bulb had to be turned on in an empty room; now they could clearly see the toll that utilities were taking on our budget.

My kids now consider putting on a sweater a viable alternative to goosing the thermostat. They understand when we pass up pricey treats at the grocery store that it is not because their parents are determined "never to have anything good to eat" as they have charged, but because we need to feed a whole family for an entire month.

Cameron's solution will not be for everyone, but since reading his account I have heard many parents describe similarly positive results with this approach. And his story is in stark contrast to the story of the eighteen-year-old who, when asked by her dad how much she thought last month's utility bill was, responded "$15,000?" This after having to be told what a utility bill is.

Families who are uncomfortable talking about money may consider Cameron's strategy a step too far, but my experience is that when given real information, kids, like anyone else, will rise to the occasion and use it wisely. The young woman who guessed that the family utility bill was $15,000 had no context for understanding, because there had been no conversations in her family to give her a clue about reality. Kids do well with reality—when they are trusted to understand and deal with it. Families whose instinct is to "protect: their children from reality are likely to experience the consequences later, when the child is reluctant to let go of the fantasyland their parents have created.

Obviously, if there is a good deal of money in family budgets that is "left over," the issues are different. But the principles are constant. Helping kids understand connections between the options they have and the choices they make is one of the most important parental tasks you can accomplish. I meet too many adults who describe, with a measure of sorrow, how hard it is to say no to the things they want and how difficult it now is to escape the chronic state of debt that comes from not being able to live within their means.

To give kids practice making choices, use the activities listed in the Life/Money Map for Stage Two (page 6), or try these:

- When your kid asks for brand-name shoes or a new high-tech toy, let him choose: "You can have X or you can get something similar but less expensive and keep the amount left over to put into your savings account."
- If your daughter wants to go to a movie, offer to put the money she would have spent into her savings account and rent a movie to watch with her instead.
- If your son's birthday is approaching, offer cash or the choice of selecting a stock he can follow that may appreciate (or decline) in value. Younger children may turn this one down, but asking the question has intrinsic value. Make the stakes bigger over time. Give your daughter the choice of going to a summer camp in another state or attending one nearer your home and donating the money you'll save on travel to a cause she cares about (Surfrider Foundation, Girl Scouts, Humane Society). Of course there is value in travel

as well, so this is not to discourage exploration, rather to encourage critical thinking.

- Are your kids spending more on apps and iTunes than you're comfortable with? Work that expenditure into their allowance and hold them to their budget. Let them know they'll need to make up the difference somewhere, and ask which they are willing to give up: eating out or movies with friends for a month?

In 1985, children aged four to twelve influenced about $50 billion of their parents' purchases each year. By 2000 that figure had quadrupled to over $200 billion. And in 2010, *Marketing Daily* claimed that teenagers had *$216 billion* in buying power. Kids are targets because companies are well aware that a nagging child can wear down a parent's resolve more effectively than an ad campaign targeting the parents, even in an era of high unemployment and in an economy still struggling to recover from the sub-prime debacle of 2008. Parental capitulation not only fills the coffers of companies but also undermines your children's ability to connect their choices with real financial consequences.

5. Introduce Role Models

Parents who share their own passions with kids offer a living role model, demonstrating that life is full of zest and wonder and that financial responsibility is part of what makes it so. Modeling the practice of budgeting support for an environmental cause or helping to keep the local health clinic open or funding a choral group you perform in is a way of helping children see you as a whole person, more than just Mom or Dad.

Being open about activities and issues that move you, and talking about those interests with kids, is a form of money talk. Whether sharing the challenges of raising money or exulting over the triumph of meeting a fund-raising goal, the conversation becomes a normal part of what kids associate with achieving something that matters deeply. By adding words like *balance sheet*, *capital*, and *budget* to their vocabulary and talking about the normal frustrations and joys of matching financial wherewithal with talent and vision, parents model the ability to talk about money comfortably.

It's a good idea to make sure kids meet—and spend time with—people who combine their passion with their vocation. If you are having friends over for dinner who fit this bill, set aside time for them to interact with your children. You don't need to interrupt all your grown-up time, but exposing kids to people who offer visions of a passionate future will expand their horizons.

Moving On

In this chapter I've discussed how to make financial issues relevant to kids in the context of their growing enthusiasms. Although attention spans are still short, and kids will lurch sometimes from powerful interest to new passion in the course of a week, it's important to remember they are just experimenting with their new world—trying it on for size. In this stage of the financial apprenticeship, the Ten Basic Money Skills can function as place markers on the journey.

In the next chapter I'll address the changing needs and attitudes of the teen who is experiencing a growing imperative to seek independence.

Messages to send in emails, hide under pillows, or stick into book bags . . .

I care about your dreams. Saving money is one way to make them come true. Love, Mom

As you develop your sense of style, let's talk about ways to look great and spend wisely too. Love, Dad

Sometimes saying no to friends is a special form of courage.

I love your idea for making hats for your friends. Go for it!

Wise women save for the future. Foolish women spend what they get. Proverbs 21:20

Imagine you have $10,000 to give away to a cause you care about. Tell me what it would be and why.

Is there an idea you have that you'd like to turn into a business? Tell me about it.

Suggest five things your dad and I can do to save money for a family vacation.

Going to school is an investment in yourself.

A social entrepreneur uses her imagination and resourcefulness to help solve problems in the community. How can you be a social entrepreneur?

I like the way you're managing your allowance—it makes me proud.

Money acts like gas in a car—it helps fuel your passions. Tell us what your passions are so we can plan how to save money to fuel yours.

"Let him step
to the music which he
hears, however
measured or far away."

HENRY DAVID THOREAU

Stage Three
Ages 13–15: Breaking Away

Stage Three is both exciting and challenging. The tensions inherent in becoming an individual with ideas and values that diverge from Mom's and Dad's make themselves felt during these years. On the one hand, teens are developing more complex and interesting personalities; on the other hand, complexity can be exhausting to manage. Just at the time you feel your kids should become more fully responsible for their financial actions, they are trying to assert their individuality at every turn—often by making it clear that what *you* want is no longer as important as *who they are becoming*.

But don't let their natural attempts at self-expression deter you from the goal: *raising financially fit kids*. Achieving this goal in the context of a turbulent developmental stage isn't easy, but this stage will pass; your children's need for a solid financial foundation will endure.

The Life/Money Map
Stage Three/Ages 13–15

Social/Emotional Development	Appropriate Money Skills to Master
Focuses primarily on the present; has only a vague sense of the future	Learns to shop comparatively
Is egocentric, self-conscious, and anxious about personal behavior	Comprehends relationship of time to money
Begins to think independently	Begins to earn money; initiates small ventures
Conforms to peer group norms and behaviors	Commits to saving goal
Tries on different roles in a highly experimental phase	Develops basic understanding of investment
	Connects money and future
	Understands philanthropy
	Decodes bank statements
	Understands interest and dividends

Flip Open

3. How to spend wisely	4. How to talk about money	5. How to live on a budget	6. How to invest
Introduce the idea of a warranty or insurance policy next time you fill one out for a purchase. efore you re-up cell phone ns, have teens search for billing options. Have choose the best plan, st being one of the reward if they can hidden fees in the y's stated price. How e taxes? How much st if they go over their ninute/text allowance? hat a hidden cost is. what an impulse buy is y candy bars are placed sh registers.	Talk about ads shown on your kids' favorite TV shows. Ask them to critique for qualities such as accuracy, honesty, and value. Tune them in—ask them to notice the financial values of friends, acquaintances, and public figures. Who do they admire? Discuss the difference between accumulation (saving) and consumption (spending). Talk about the environmental and human implications of each.	If you haven't already, now's the time to take your child to the bank and open a checking account. Give her her allowance by check to deposit, and plan regular trips to the bank so she can perform the transactions herself. Show her your own budget. Ask for advice. Whether you use a pen and paper or software, sharing your budget shows teens you respect them and take them seriously. Have your teen plan and budget for a family outing. Put her in charge of everything required for a full day, including gas, food, tips, and entry fees. Give her cash at the start of the day. If she runs out before the day is over, don't bail her out; go home early and try the exercise again in a month. Go beyond needs = good, wants = bad. Ask independent-minded kids to spend, save, and give in a way that reflects their best selves.	When you come across an about the companies beh your teen's favorite brand him to read them and tell whether he feels the com nies sound like risks or sc investment possibilities. Introduce the idea of impa investing. Ask your child t research and track three companies (preferably th making products he uses) let you know which is the socially responsible and w thinks so (see the Resour for research tools). Buy stock in a company t has meaning to your teen, review the annual report w him, and visit the compan website for interim news.
ite comparison sites: Google Product indthebest.com, .com naire Next Door: rising Secrets of s Wealthy, Thomas J. and William D. Danko er Reports website: nsumerreports.org	*What You Owe Me*, Bebe Moore Campbell *Teen Talk: Money: How to Get It . . . Keep It . . . Avoid Getting Ripped Off!*, William R. Hegeman Money Management International turned a survey about how kids spend into a graphic that can spark conversation:bit.ly/IMI _ SeptSpending	An education program that stimulates learning about economics and finance: www.smg2000.org	*When I Grow Up I'm Going Be a Millionaire (A Childre Guide to Mutual Funds)*, Ted Lea and Lora Lea A publication for environmentally friendly investing and business: www.greenmoneyjournal. www.tipsforkids.com *The Teenage Investor*, Timothy Olsen Camp Start-Up: www.independentmeans.c imi/camp-start-up

Financial candor, like an

expectation of good manners, should

be part of daily family life.

w to exercise the preneurial spirit	8. How to handle credit	9. How to use money to change the world.	10. How to be a citizen of the world.
your teen a biography entrepreneur. est that your child er friends run a borhood car wash to money to buy holiday your kid an email nformation about a ess plan competition an enter.	Don't give pre-paid credit cards as training wheels. Kids end up paying through the nose for the privilege of using their own money. Better to set up checking accounts with debit cards or give cash gifts. If you carry a balance, give your child your credit card bills and ask him to tell you how much you are spending each month on interest. Ask your child to go online and see if he can find a credit card that would charge lower interest than your current card. If he finds a better deal, make the switch. Explain what a credit report is.	While teens are still figuring out what their priorities are, encourage them to do one-day projects. A day off from school can be the incentive that helps them find their philanthropic passion. On Valentine's Day, give your teen $50 to make a contribution to a cause that's "close to her heart." Make a contribution to Emily's List in your daughter's name. Gather their friends or siblings for an afternoon as a mini-grant-making board. Give them a moderate amount and let them decide how to use it to make a difference.	Take advantage of aspirational tastes and give them a subscription to the Italian edition of *Vogue*, the German edition of *Auto Motor und Sport*, or a subscription to the *Economist* for their next birthday.
ompany: The Money with Attitude, ble through the store at www endentmeans.com oss: Running the Like the Big Chicks, y Kravetz n American oreneurs, askins	*Credit Card Nation: The Consequences of America's Addiction to Credit*, Robert D. Manning	www.emilyslist.org *Volunteer Vacations: Short-Term Adventures That Will Benefit You and Others*, Bill McMillon, Doug Cutchins, and Ann Geissinger Cause World and the Extraordinaires are free iPhone apps for social networking and philanthropy. Metowe.com engages young people in changing the world through blogs, speakers, volunteer trips, and fashion. *Catch the Spirit: Teen Volunteers Tell How They Made a Difference*, Susan K. Perry	www.globegenie.com uses Google Maps to "teleport" you to somewhere random in the world.

The Ten Basic Money Skills

This time around, the Ten Basic Money Skills activities will be used to support and reinforce the connections between independence and responsibility, giving kids tools to shape themselves into people with depth and substance.

	Basic Money Skill	
	1. How to save	2. How to get paid what you're worth
Actions: 13–15 Years	Find a goal connected to independence and set an expectation for your child's contribution to it. Whether it's for owning a car in a couple of years or going on a class trip, some of the money for this undertaking can come from a dedicated savings plan. Send a message: financial planning equals independence.	Ask your money mentoring team what work for pay they may be able to offer your teen.
		For kids too young to work, skill-building summer experiences trump the summer doldrums. Sign them up for computer classes, practice interviewing, introduce basic business language.
	Show teens that shopping isn't just for clothes by offering $50 if they can find a savings account that has the most free features.	Send this email to your teen "Salary comes from Latin word *salarium*, meaning 'allowance.' Roman soldiers given a salarium as part of their income." Remind y that she is blessed not to Roman soldier!
	Write a letter (or an email) to your child. Discuss your own experience with learning (or not learning) to save and the effect it has had on your life and independence.	Give your kid a list of ten and ask him to search for average pay of each on th Internet (see sidebar on page 99 for job suggestio Ask him to find entry-lev salaries and salaries for s with ten years' experience
	Revisit the concept of compound interest. Explain that while interest rates are low currently, they are still an important part of a healthy savings plan.	
Resources	*20 $ecrets to Money and Independence: The DollarDiva's Guide to Life*, Joline Godfrey	Job-finding websites wit lots of info and resource www.monster.com and www.careerbuilder.com
	Countdown to a Thousand Dollars, Lisa Kerber	One Day One Job is a we that each day looks at w it's like to be an employe intern) at a cool company www.onedayonejob.com
	www.yacenter.org	A complete online course babysitting: www.baby sittingclass.com

Financial literacy is not

just about the money

but about launching great kids.

Big Tasks for Stage Three

The big tasks in this stage include

1. Revisiting the Ten Basic Money Skills in a yet more sophisticated fashion, holding kids accountable for their financial behavior
2. Helping teens make the connection between financial responsibility and personal independence
3. Stretching their vision into the future
4. Providing experiences and opportunities to grow beyond the self-absorption of their age
5. Tuning into warning signs that your child is not developing sound financial skills and intervening as necessary

I. The Ten Basic Money Skills, Round Three

This time around, the Ten Basic Money Skills activities will be used to support and reinforce the connections between independence and responsibility, giving kids tools to shape themselves into people with depth and substance.

2. Making Connections Between Financial Responsibility and Personal Independence

Years ago I met with officers of the Salvation Army to explore ways to integrate financial literacy skills into programs they offer. The captain I spoke with said, "We are concerned about the spiritual well-being of the people who come to us, but if we do not also help them develop skills to stand on their own, we are letting them down. Providing financial literacy is akin to giving people the skill to fish rather than handing them fish to eat." This leader's goal was to teach people to make the connection between learning basic financial skills and taking care of themselves.

Across the economic spectrum, the desire to help kids develop into well-rounded people who contribute to family and community is universal. And although many parents would love to see their kids live on Easy Street, the fact is that families who rob kids of the opportunity to develop skills of independence do them a great disservice—not just in the short term, but in the long run as well.

Moving the Conversation to a Higher Plane

By now teens know—or at least intuit—that money equals independence. The mantra for allowances set forth earlier (see page 47) is now joined by a corollary: *the more financially responsible you are, the more independence you will earn.* (Give teens a T-shirt with this motto printed on the back if you think it will help!)

These are the years when teenagers start dating, go places with friends without parental supervision, travel, stay home alone, make decisions for themselves, and experiment with new tastes and experiences. Too often, conversation about these opportunities and adventures turns into a fractious tug-of-war that has more to do with authority and control than with the issue of independence it is really about.

Writing for the journal *More than Money*, Ann Slepian demonstrated how to move the discourse with your kids to a higher level:

> When I say "No" to something my son wants to buy or do, I've coached him to ask me, "What will help?" I then think out loud: "Well, on the one hand, I want you to learn how to budget your money and save for the things you really want. That's a really important skill in life, one that many adults don't know well enough. That's one reason I ask you to rethink the need to spend money on this {trip, item, etc.}. On the other hand, it's something that may help you grow as a person, and I'd be willing to pay half the cost if you really want it. But I will want you to pay me back if you don't use the money well and wisely."
>
> Sometimes, by thinking out loud, I find creative ways to address whatever concerns I really have about the request that led me to say no initially. Other times it seems nothing will help. The answer is still no. He's still mad at me, but he can see I'm not just being an arbitrary authority.

Shifting the level of discourse from a war of wills to a collaboration in search of a solution models the power of problem solving. It is also the most effective way to help teens develop good judgment in service of their own independence. Along the lines of "What would help?" you might try these approaches:

How will this trip, action, or choice affect your budget, savings account, plans for the future, checking account? Getting teens to make the connection between choices and financial impact is a habit best learned when they have something at stake. For example, suppose you've already created a financial plan for the year with your teen, when a new opportunity crops up. Whether or not you can easily afford to fund the unexpected event is less impor- tant than that you review the opportunity with him in light of the plan already in place: Is there something he can give up later in the year? Is there a way to earn some extra money to make sure the budget is balanced at the end of the year? The challenge of managing spontaneity, unexpected opportunity, and finite resources is constant throughout life, whether your kid becomes a teacher in an inner-city school, the head of a nonprofit, the head of a household, the CEO of an Inc. 500 company, or the leader of a country.

How can you demonstrate that you have the judgment and discipline to make a good financial decision? Going on a backpacking trip in one of the national parks with one's friends, without an adult along, may not seem to have much to do with money at the planning stage, but getting your teen to contemplate the question is a way to help him explore the connection. Ask: Are you using your own money for entrance fees, food, travel expenses, and equipment? Is that how you want to spend your money? What will you have to economize on later if you do this now? By now your teen may be earning money from a part-time or summer job. Or maybe he's begun to receive funds from a trust fund or has a generous aunt who occasionally slips him extra cash. Whatever his source of funds, it is wise to have him handle larger and larger shares of his spending budgets. This will provide practice for managing a greater scale, later in life.

3. Focus on the Future

For thirteen- to fifteen-year-olds, the future isn't quite as far away as it once was. Though this age may be characterized by an exaggerated focus on self and only a vague awareness of the future, this is the time when helping kids dream big and expanding their vision of possibilities becomes even more important.

Lifestyle Budgeting: A Practice Session

Give her a peek at her future with this lifestyle activity, which can be done at home or as part of a teen gathering:

1. First ask each teen to select a profession, job, or venture that will provide income. Make no judgments or comments about their selections.
2. Next have teens search the Web for the average entry-level income for that choice. The Bureau of Labor Statistics (www.bls.gov/bls/blswage.htm) is helpful for this exercise.
3. Have them note the salary on a piece of paper. (Call it a balance sheet.)
4. Now ask them to make some lifestyle choices. The sample budget on pages 100–102 will get them started. Note that the numbers are national averages

for a single person living alone and are hypothetical for the purpose of this activity. You can make the numbers more meaningful by researching figures for your particular region of the country—or better yet, have the kids do that.

Once teens have made their selections, have them fill in the Budget Worksheet on page 103. For many kids this is a lightning-bolt insight. The very concept of "entry level" is alien to kids who have been taught by reality TV that stardom and wealth are instant attainments.

In the workshops we run using a version of this activity, we see as many individual reactions and solutions as there are kids. One young woman who yearned to be an actress was startled to find that a first-year, entry-level actress *might* make $4,000 per year. When she saw that her lifestyle choices included owning a house and driving an SUV, she got very practical about what she would need to do if she really intended to pursue her dream. She eventually decided to get an MBA and pursue entertainment management rather than give up her lifestyle aspirations. Of course, scaling back on the desire for an SUV and a Neiman Marcus charge card is another strategy—one worth exploring with kids in the context of family financial values.

Giving kids a chance to "practice their fantasies" in some reality-based way may feel like throwing cold water on their dreams, but you're *not* helping them to expand their visions in ways that allow them to attain real independence could cheat them of a full, secure, and satisfying future.

Cool Jobs

Animator
Dolphin trainer
Audio engineer
Marine biologist
Neurotechnology scientist
State senator
Television producer
Demographer
Hotel general manager
Botanist
Magazine editor
Broadway theater manager
Vineyard manager
Currency trader
Family law attorney
Sierra Club lawyer
Grade-school teacher
College professor
Archaeologist
Astronomer
Detective
Sports agent

Sample Lifestyle Budget		
Housing	Renter (two-bedroom apartment) Average monthly rent:	$1,600
	Home Owner (costs include mortgage payment, property taxes, insurance, repairs) Average total monthly cost:	$2,000
Saving and Investment	Minimal Investor Monthly contribution:	$50
	Moderate Investor Monthly contribution:	$200
	Future Millionaire Monthly contribution:	$1,000
Food	Thrifty Spender (cooks at home, shops for sales, and sticks to a budget) Average monthly cost:	$150
	Moderate Spender (cooks at home, including some gourmet food, but occasionally splurges on a meal in a nice restaurant) Average monthly cost:	$350
	Big Spender (cooks gourmet and eats out often) Average monthly cost:	$500
Utilities	Home Owner (pays all monthly utilities, including gas, electric, fuel oil, water, and sewer) Average monthly cost:	$350
	Apartment Renter (pays electricity only) Average monthly cost:	$85
Health Care	Copayments, services, and prescriptions Average monthly cost:	$150
	Taking a pass on health care: Average monthly cost:	$0

Sample Lifestyle Budget		
Clothing	Thrifty Spender (shops at second-hand stores and sales and sticks to a budget) Average monthly cost:	$60
	Medium Spender (shops at Gap, Express, Sears, and J.C. Penney) Average monthly cost:	$160
	Big Spender (buys designer clothes and shops at boutiques) Average monthly cost:	$500+
Transportation	Public Transportation Average monthly cost:	$50
	New Car (financed zero down, 8 percent APR for 36 months; tax and license fees not included) 2013 Honda Civic, monthly payment: 2013 Ford Explorer, monthly payment: 2013 BMW X6, monthly payment:	$463 $753 $1,540
	Used Car 2007 Nissan Sentra, monthly payment: 2009 Ford F-150, monthly payment: 2005 Scion xA, monthly payment:	$278 $500 $220
Car Operations	Average Mileage Driver (12,000 miles per year, with car insurance and repairs) Average monthly cost:	$600
	Heavy Mileage Driver (24,000 miles per year, with car insurance and repairs) Average monthly cost:	$750
Home Furnishing and Supplies	New Home Furnishings (IKEA style) Average monthly cost:	$300
	Used Home Furnishings (thrift store purchases) Average monthly cost:	$125
	Raiding the Family Attic: Average monthly cost:	$0

Sample Lifestyle Budget		
Phone Service	Basic Monthly Service Average monthly cost:	$40
	Bells and Whistles Average monthly cost:	$100
Cable TV	Basic Monthly Service (limited basic) Average monthly cost:	$30
	Every Conceivable Station (digital) Average monthly cost:	$145
Internet Service	Basic Monthly Service (dial-up) Average monthly cost:	$15
	Broadband Access (DSL) Average monthly cost:	$55
Entertainment	Thrifty Spender (rents movies, attends free concerts, frequents parks and libraries) Average monthly cost:	$75
	Medium Spender (goes to movies, local concerts, and sports events about once a week) Average monthly cost:	$150
	Big Spender (attends big-name concerts, big-ticket sports events, and the theater) Average monthly cost:	$350

Teen's Budget Worksheet		
Your Career	**Enter Net Monthly Salary**	$
Housing	Enter Monthly Mortgage or Rent	$
Savings and Investment	Enter Savings and Investment Contributions	$
Food	Enter Montly Food Costs	$
Utilities	Enter Monthly Utilities Costs	$
Health Care	Enter Monthly Health Care Costs	$
Clothing	Enter Monthly Clothing Costs	$
Transportation	Enter Monthly Transportation Costs	$
Car Operations	Enter Monthly Costs to Drive a Car (enter $0 if you chose public transportation)	$
Home Furnishings and Supplies	Enter Monthly Home Furnishings Costs	$
Phone Service	Enter Monthly Cell Phone Costs	$
Cable TV	Enter Monthly Cable TV Costs	$
Internet Service	Enter Monthly Internet Costs	$
Entertainment	Enter Monthly Entertainment Costs	$
1. Add up all of your monthly costs and enter the total in the box to the right.	**Total Monthly Cost =**	$
2. Now subtract your Total Monthly Costs from your Monthly Net Salary (first box). This amount is your Final Balance.	**Final Balance =**	$

Lifestyle Budgeting: Real Life

The following table is geared toward helping teens create a lifestyle budget for their present real life. Each category has two percentages, the first indicating what part of the budget the teen will be responsible for from her allowance and other income and the second representing the percentage the parent will handle. Amounts for the allowance should be disbursed monthly or quarterly, depending on the teen's readiness to handle income. You may have to experiment a bit to assess true readiness—the goal is to have the teen handling a budget of a three- to six-month duration by the time she's out of this stage of development.

Percentages listed are recommended only; you'll need to create your own formulas for your family. You may decide that in some of the categories you will contribute nothing; in some you will cover all of the expenses.

Clothing: This share percentage may change every six to twelve months. The more responsibility your kid has, the greater your responsibility not to give in to regular requests for extras. This is a learning exercise. If you want the right to splurge or to give a gift, do so, but acknowledge it as a special event—a windfall, not a regular occurrence.

Entertainment: The simple act of getting teens to estimate how many recreational activities and purchases they want to engage in over the course of a one- to three-month period will be a new experience for them. And tallying the total cost of those decisions will be a revelation. With some kids, this is the easiest budget category to make into a learning experience. If your teenager wants to see three movies a month but spends his money on other things before getting to the third movie, he'll have an instant "behavior has consequences" experience without you having to offer a single word of reproach. The learning, of course, will only happen *if you do not bail him out.* The point is to help teens live with consequences when the stakes are not life-and-death. This is a lot easier when he is thirteen than when he is twenty-five or forty-five.

Transportation: Even if you pay for 98 percent of transportation, being aware of the cost involved (gas, car maintenance, airfare, bus fare) is an important lesson for a teen. Asking her to contribute even 2 percent from her allowance puts the cost on her radar. And if it is transportation to ballet, riding lessons, or football practice, all the more reason to be aware of the costs.

Categories	Child / Parent Percentages	Amount per Month
Clothing	70/30	
Entertainment	70/30	
Transportation	10/90	
Education	10/90	
Food	20/80	
Hobbies	40/60	
Special Events	30/70	
Savings	50/50	
Philanthropy	80/20	

Education: Both private and public schools, in an attempt to trim budgets, are requiring families to cover an ever-wider range of school materials and activities. Again, you may cover 99 percent of all education costs for your teen, but letting her know the costs will clue her in to the investment being made in her future—and if she has aspirations to start a school of her own someday, she'll have a sense of what is involved.

Food: This is another category in which the notion that behavior has consequences can be reinforced. Does your son's money go to vending machines and french fries? If he isn't exercising some degree of control and moderation over his food habits, you can tie percentage increases in this part of the budget to improvements in his diet.

Hobbies: Whether she plays soccer or collects comic books, an estimate of the expenses involved in these activities (including registration fees, trips, and purchases) will help her appreciate what it means to be able to invest money in a passion. If training for a place on the WNBA or a slot in the Winter Olympics is part of her dream, then uniforms, lessons, and coaches should be included in this category.

Special Events: You can't always anticipate a special event, but you can assume there will be some, so it's possible to allocate a certain amount annually to cover the possibilities. And if this is the year of the bat or bar mitzvah, or some other rite of passage, factor that in as well.

Savings: Deducting a certain amount from each allowance payment is one way to get in the habit of saving. This should be nonnegotiable. If your kids have not yet gotten in the habit of putting savings aside by themselves, introduce them to the mechanism of the automatic deduction and simply withhold an agreed-upon part of the allowance to deposit in their bank accounts. Including them in the decision of where to place their savings is another way of demonstrating there are many ways to save. Does he want to put the money in a bank CD or use a credit union? Open an account at a savings bank? Invest in Treasury bills? Asking teenagers to research where their money will make the most money is one way to engage them in the decision-making process.

Philanthropy: Philanthropy is a powerful way of connecting teens to something larger than themselves. By Stage Three, they should be able to make enlightened choices about how and where to share "time, treasure, and talent." During lean months, suggest offering time or talent in lieu of money.

By the time you and your teen tally up the total amount of her budget, it may look like an enormous amount of money—in fact it may *be* an enormous amount of money. But putting the numbers on paper is one way to reveal the hidden cost of family life—as well as to illuminate the real choices you make in managing the larger family budget. If you're raising kids to shepherd wealth responsibly, early practice is critical; if your family has been hit by a bad economy or an illness and you need everyone to pull together, shared information and collaboration is essential to helping kids feel secure and included in family solutions.

Parents often withhold information to "protect" their kids. This may have the unintended consequence of triggering anxiety in young people whose imaginings create far more distressing realities than actually exist. Financial candor can and should be a part of family life, like parents' expectation of good manners or clarity about curfews.

Reactivating the Money Mentoring Team

These are the years when I urge parents to "trade their kids." That is, it may be easier for your daughter to hear some things from her best friend's mom than from you. And your son's best friend may be more comfortable getting financial guidance in your house than in his own. Now is the time to reactivate the money mentoring team. (If you've just entered the book in this chapter, see chapter 2 for information about assembling a money mentoring team.)

Assuming the arrangement has worked thus far, send your money mentors a note asking them to renew their agreement for another couple of years. (You may also add new members.) Give them an update on your teen and his or her current goals. Reciprocity is key; your money mentor, like you, is likely to have a full life. Make sure you offer a gift certificate to dinner, an overnight stay for their kids at your house, or an equally meaningful gesture. Then ask the money mentor to

- Share how her career unfolded. Is she doing what she thought she would be doing? What does she enjoy in her work? What does she wish someone had told her when she was fourteen?
- Take teens to meetings (a business meeting, city council meeting, club meeting) where adults are talking, planning, and considering ideas that relate to financial choices and decisions.
- Share podcasts and books that offer ideas for their future (I love Goodreads and Shelfari for this).
- Include teens in projects to which they might make a contribution.

This is the stage in which you can suggest that teens select their own money mentoring team. What do they want to learn, and how will they recruit adults to teach them? Kids can be effective in assembling their own mentors—and adults are often flattered to have been selected by teenagers. Whether your teen approaches the owner of a local business, the manager of a brokerage firm, or the executive director of United Way, she may be more successful than you in getting them to sign on as a money mentor.

Teens as Financial Futurists

Another strategy for helping teenagers envision the future involves their friends. As part of a party or a sleepover, ask teens to come prepared to create a "mural of the future." Provide a giant piece of paper, markers, and lots of space to work in. Then ask them to draw three visions of the future (each to include where they'll live, what they'll be doing, who they'll hang out with, what they'll be achieving): (1) a wild imagining of what might happen; (2) the scenario that's the most likely; and (3) a worst-case scenario (believe me, it's already in their heads—you're just putting it on the table, so to speak).

Once they have their pictures complete, give them time to explain their depictions. Now ask them to revisit the mural and think about what it means financially:

- What will each scenario cost?
- Where will the money come from?
- How important is it for them to actively build that future? How might they do that?
- What do they need to do to prevent the worst-case scenario from happening, and what might they do to ensure the best case?

4. Starting to Think Outside the Self

Whether they are fully aware or not, teens are now identifying with current issues, worrying about the plight of a friend, or identifying with a character in a film or book as they evolve beyond pure self-interest. But getting them to think about money in a larger context means seeing themselves as part of the economic web of the community and of the nation.

Teenagers are intuitively, if not consciously, aware that they and their friends help drive the economy. Indeed, they are likely to be quite aware that films, toys, high-tech products, clothes, sports equipment, and almost everything else they put their hands on are marketed to them aggressively—but that is not the same as understanding one's place in the economic web of the community.

Seeing oneself as an *actor* as opposed to simply being acted upon is a vastly different perspective for the financial apprentice. One way to help your teen make this shift is to create a visual representation. You can complete the following chart with your teen to illustrate the impact he has on the financial life of the community. Point out that the number of high schools and dollars spent on constructing or renovating schools are directly related to how many school-aged students live in your town and how education for teens is prioritized in your community. You can point out that tax dollars are spent to make sure your son and his friends have access to summer recreation activities, a police force to provide security, and bike paths on which to ride safely. Ask your daughter whether she's happy with the way her community regards the place of teenagers in the economic web—and if not, what would she like done differently? Ask your son to tally up the services in the community designed specifically for him and his peers.

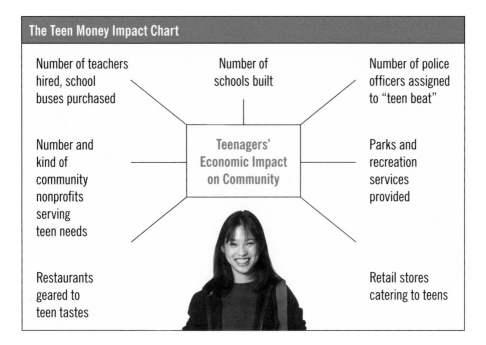

The Teen Money Impact Chart

Number of teachers hired, school buses purchased

Number of schools built

Number of police officers assigned to "teen beat"

Number and kind of community nonprofits serving teen needs

Teenagers' Economic Impact on Community

Parks and recreation services provided

Restaurants geared to teen tastes

Retail stores catering to teens

Teens' Economic Impact

Becoming aware of themselves in the wider context of a community can give kids a vital feeling of connectedness. You might build on this sensibility by taking a walking tour of your town or neighborhood and pointing out the parts of the community on which kids have an impact, such as

- The number of schools built
- The number of school buses purchased
- The number of teachers hired

- The kinds of parks and recreational resources provided, such as a skateboard park, tennis courts, or a public swimming pool
- The success—or lack thereof—of stores that target teenagers as customers
- The size of churches and other houses of worship that are built
- The kinds of services offered by the local library

If this walking tour engenders a realization that the community is *not* putting money into services or facilities that make young people's lives better, the experience can trigger a sense of righteous outrage that will encourage some kids to become activists for their peers.

Youth Activism as an Element of Financial Literacy

Activism among young kids is a great way to help them achieve an awareness of the world outside the self, asking "What does this mean for other kids in the community? In other countries?" Much has been changed by the force of a child's passion. Who can forget ten-year-old Samantha Smith, the little girl from Maine who had the moxie to write a letter to Soviet General Secretary Yuri Andropov expressing her fear of nuclear war between his nation and the United States? That letter put into play a whole series of events that took Samantha to the (then) Soviet Union to meet with Andropov. Today, Waging Peace (www.wagingpeace.org) is an internationally recognized nonprofit organization that emerged from the vision of this little girl.

Similarly, Kids Can Free the Children (www.freethechildren.org) was started by a twelve-year-old in 1995. Craig Kielburger was searching for the comics in his local paper when he noticed an article about a young Pakistani boy who had been sold into bondage as a carpet weaver. Though the boy escaped, he was later murdered for speaking out against child labor. Moved by the boy's story, Craig rallied some friends and founded the organization Kids Can Free the Children.

Now a thirty-something young man, Kielburger has traveled worldwide to speak out in defense of children's rights, meeting with such figures as the Dalai Lama, Mother Teresa, and Pope John Paul II. The nonprofit organization he started has grown to involve more than a hundred thousand young people in over thirty-five countries. These young philanthropists have been responsible for the distribution of approximately 100,000 health and school kits and in excess of $16 million worth of medical supplies to needy families in the developing world (when I wrote the first edition of this book ten years ago, this was "just" $2.5 million!).

Your kids may not launch a worldwide organization, but empowering them to have an impact on other people's lives is an important step in their developing competence and self-worth. Kids who understand their part in the economic web of the world tend to make more thoughtful decisions for their own lives—as well as for the larger community.

More Great Nonprofits Started by Kids

The Victorian Hands Foundation
Nadia Campbell started this intergenerational elder appreciation organization after watching a television special on elder abuse and neglect when she was eighteen. (tvhf.org)

Kids Helping Kids
After being diagnosed with a brain tumor, thirteen-year-old Mischa Zimmerman established a volunteer organization that lets teens and children take action to help kids affected by catastrophic illness and injury. (kidshelping.org)

Kids Konnected
Eleven-year-old Jon Wagner-Holtz started this support organization when he couldn't find any other kids to talk to after his mother was diagnosed with breast cancer. (kidskonnected.org)

Grandma's Gifts
Nine-year-old Emily Douglas established this nonprofit in memory of her grandmother, to raise money and gather donations for organizations in Appalachian Ohio. (grandmasgifts.org)

Lauri Slavitt, a mom and a principal in a Silicon Valley foundation, relates this story:

> *Daniel (five) and Jordana (six) decided to start a business called the Key to Hope to help underprivileged children in the Bay Area. They began making special key chains in different designs. Each key chain takes an hour to make. They began by selling them to friends and family, but the key chains were beautiful, and several people suggested they sell them at local supermarkets and community fairs. The kids ended up getting space at fairs and were allowed to solicit outside our local supermarket. Some people bought the key chains and then donated extra because they saw how earnest the kids were. The orders were coming in at such a rapid rate (special flags, individual*

designs, and the like), they decided to get up an hour early before school each day and do at least three at night. This business lasted for over one year, and they made a total of $1,000. Most of the key chains sold for $3.00. They are now in the process of researching places to donate these monies.

Daniel and Jordana began "making a difference" well before adolescence, and there is a good chance their engagement with the community will have an inoculating effect against teenage cynicism. These kids have taken action, have been taken seriously, and are now engaged in a process that extends well beyond a simple empathic response to the needs of other kids.

5. Caveat: The Dark Side of Financial Literacy

I would be remiss to talk about kids as though they are all children of June and Ward Cleaver, waiting eagerly for adult wisdom about issues of money and business. Money offers as much opportunity for wayward antics as any other part of kids' lives, and super-achieving young people with an abundance of resourcefulness and opportunity can be financially sophisticated and get themselves in a peck of trouble very easily.

Possible Concerns

The clever child who pushes the envelope to see what he can get away with (aka "the hustler"). Testing limits as they search for "the rules," these teens may just be looking for something to do—in which case, helping them find ways to fill idle time is worth your while. Kids who are not shown clear ethics and boundaries relative to money may fall into habits that can get them into trouble with friends, employers, and the IRS later in life.

The independent child whose parents are sure everything is fine but don't push far enough to confirm that reality. Included in this group are parents who abdicate their role as overseer because they think, "My child is smart and knows what he's doing." Possibly the most dramatic example of this behavior was the Internet investing adventures of Jonathan Lebed, entertainingly reported some years ago by Michael Lewis in an article for the *New York Times*.

Jonathan was described as a sullen, withdrawn fifteen-year-old who figured out how to reinvent himself online into a brash, confident internet-savvy stockbroker. He and his friends mastered the art of the Internet message board, hyping stocks online, watching them climb in price, and selling at impressive (if overheated) profits.

Eventually, Jonathan accumulated over $800,000 in Internet stock profits, was investigated by the SEC (before whom his lawyer argued, fairly legitimately, that Jonathan's techniques were no different from those of many Wall Street analysts), and eventually was forced to return $300,000 in the form of fines. Lewis leaves the reader to decide for him- or herself whether or not Jonathan did anything wrong. (That some of those analysts Jonathan's lawyer referred to have now been charged with crimes makes it a little less ambiguous.) But Lewis does shed light on how it happened:

> *Greg and Connie {Jonathan's parents} were born in New Jersey, but from the moment the Internet struck, they might as well have just arrived from Taiwan. When the Internet landed on them, it redistributed the prestige and authority that goes with a general understanding of the ways of the world away from the grown-ups and to the child. The grown-ups now depended on the child to translate for them. Technology had turned them into a family of immigrants. "I know, I know," Greg said, turning to me. "I'm supposed to know how it works. It's the future. But that's his future, not mine!"*

Lewis makes the point that in abdicating knowledge of what Jonathan was actually up to at all hours, the parents provided ripe ground for his financial crimes. Indeed, computer-savvy kids who can reinvent themselves as anonymous adults online have ample opportunity to play out what otherwise might be adolescent antics, with substantially higher risks and consequences.

The cynic. Another emerging concern is the tendency toward cynicism that arises when young people discover that the world, already confusing, does not necessarily improve with the acquisition or control of money. In decades of meetings with kids from around the United States and other countries, I've been struck by their awareness that money alone doesn't make the world a better place or make people any happier. To some extent, existential angst has always been a part of the teen experience. But the more worldly teen coming of age in the global economy sees tangibly that pain and suffering flow from unethical dealings with massive sums of money—whether it's the personal loss of home, a parent's loss of a job, hardship in the life of a friend whose family has suffered a financial reversal, or some other social disruption.

Possible Solution

What can you do if you see these symptoms in your kids? Here are four interventions to try.

Take time. Unchallenged views grow insidiously. Lectures won't help—but conversation, real and often, can do wonders. Demonstrating the power of one, of personal involvement—volunteering at a soup kitchen or participating in another activity that has a real effect on your community—can have an even stronger impact. Insist on finding a way to make a difference with teenagers in your life. It is an active way to challenge youthful attitudes about how hopeless the world is.

Develop your own rotating internship program. If a teenager is disillusioned with the world, one role model may not be enough; some kids require a *critical mass* of role models. One person making a difference may be an anomaly, but ten role models constitute a reality shift. Enroll friends and colleagues for active duty. Friends who have responsibilities in community-based programs (the more grassroots, the better) or socially responsible businesses can each offer a day to host a young person. If each of ten friends offers to play host one month, each teen will have a shot at seeing how at least ten people view the possibilities of changing the world. Your son or daughter may argue about the true impact these role models are making, but if so, they will have the very real experience of arguing with adults outside the family circle who can and will take them seriously. With any luck, one or more of these adults will connect with the teen on a meaningful level.

Insist on action. This may sound obvious, but even the most world-weary child needs adult-imposed expectations. Perhaps your teen despairs about how little things matter, but allowing that worldview to be indulged without insisting that they test their assumptions does a disservice to their development. Young people don't want to believe that nothing matters, but if you don't require involvement with something greater than themselves, they will be left to their own cynical beliefs.

Leverage peer power. Is there an event or activity you can invite their friends to participate in? If you arrange for ten kids to volunteer as a group at a local animal shelter or you recruit all your child's friends to throw a holiday party for a group of foster kids, you can harness the power of group learning. Although these "micro" actions will not solve the larger question of how to change the world, they will get kids talking and thinking about questions of micro versus macro change—a vast improvement over change versus no change.

Cynicism is a form of self-protection. Professed hopelessness gives kids an excuse to avoid risks. As grown-ups, we know that growth comes primarily through the process of taking risks, failing, learning, and trying again. Kids need to be drawn into experiences of risk taking—and if not when they are young, when the stakes are lower, then when? If children are not encouraged and pushed and bullied and lured into risk taking by parents and grandparents, then by whom?

Many adults, worldly as we have become, may feel that there is legitimacy to a child's despair. We can hardly bear the front-page news of the day. Yet this makes it even more important to offer kids reasons for growing up, and instruction on how to employ money as a force for good. Adults usually have the counterbalancing knowledge that people who strive for a better world get both personal and existential satisfaction from the quest, and the direct knowledge that indeed one person can make a difference. Kids need the adults in their lives to offer challenges to their half-formed ideas. It's part of your job as a grown-up.

Moving On

Closing this chapter with a cautionary word about the dark side of financial awareness is not meant to take anything away from the wonder of this stage of the financial apprenticeship. Taking steps toward independence is a form of primal optimism. It is a way the child has of saying "Yes! I can do this—I can be my own person." These teen years are a prime time for the emergence of a new independence. As we will see in the next chapter, an increased mastery of the Ten Basic Money Skills provides teens with the self-confidence required to make a successful transition from child to young adult.

"You've got to do your own growing, no matter how tall your grandfather was."

IRISH PROVERB

Chapter 6

Stage Four
Ages 16–18: Standing Tall

Breaking away now leads the confident teen to a posture of "standing tall." These are years in which teens begin to feel a genuine sense of self. They have less anxiety about the process of separation from their parents and are eager to pursue their own vision of the future: leaving home for college, starting a career, entering the public service sphere, trekking through India, or other life choices. One vehicle for this level of confidence is trusting oneself—and being trusted—to be financially competent.

Throughout this book, I emphasize that financial education is not just about the money. Financial competency is, in the best sense, a tool that enables young people to manifest their values, their character, and their substance. It's a means of demonstrating self-reliance and discipline— in short, a way of playing out the essence of who they are and who they will become.

The Life/Money Map
Stage Four/Ages 16–18

Social/Emotional Development	Appropriate Money Skills to Master
Has increased capacity for logical thought and planning	Actively saves, spends, invests
Is preoccupied with acceptance by peer group	Connects goals and saving
Experiments with independence	Experiences responsibility for self and others
Confronts serious life and moral decisions	Is able to talk about money and plan future
	Understands money as power
	Can read a paycheck, do simple tax forms
	Shows developing capacity for economic self-sufficiency

Flip Open

3. How to spend wisely	4. How to talk about money	5. How to live on a budget	6. How to invest
Give a lesson on tipping: when and how much. Take your teen with you to buy the next family car, computer, entertainment center, or other big-ticket item, then let her research, choose, and go with you to purchase the next big item after that. If you let your kid have a cell phone, ask her to recommend three different billing options, showing which is the most cost-effective. Question their devotion to labels and causes. Ask them: how does how you spend represent what you believe? Ask often. Even if they don't know now, the question will stick for years.	Discuss the family estate plans: talk about wills and other legal documents your kids should know about in case of an emergency. Discuss dating etiquette and how your son or daughter can handle the issue of who spends money for what on dates. Ask your teen to list his top five money worries and then ask him to come up with a plan for reducing his anxiety. Have your teen write budgets for three to five rites of passage such as a prom, wedding, or other celebration. Before each milestone (driver's license, graduation), require them to write down one goal for the next six months.	If you haven't already, move your teen up to a quarterly or annual allowance, on the condition that they show you proof that they've tracked expenses for a month. When your teen starts her first job, don't fill her tax forms out for her—fill them out *with* her, explaining taxes. Ask your teen to fill out her own college financial aid forms. Let her interview you for the information she needs. Give your teen three hypothetical annual incomes of $23,000, $65,000, and $150,000. Ask her to create a budget for each lifestyle. Remind her to figure in taxes, savings, and philanthropy. The family car is a great vehicle for (re)introducing money management Before handing over the keys, spend at least an hour on financial driver's ed.	To remind your teen what a bond is, you can explain that the word comes from the early English word *ba* meaning a fastening. In investing terminology, a b implies that one is bound repay an obligation. Set up a time for your kid to meet with your financia advisor to talk about wha advisor's role is. Take your teen to an annu meeting. Give your teen a subscript to the *GreenMoney Journa*
Teen Consumer Scrapbook of informational articles: www.atg.wa.gov Learn about the holistic worldview of the LOHAS Consumer, comprising environmental concerns, human health, and human rights: www.lohasjournal.com *No Impact Man* (documentary and book), Colin Beavan	*Wreck This Journal*, Keri Smith	The online game Celebrity Calamity skews a bit young but lets teens practice tracking money while managing a whiny celebrity's money: http://financialentertainment.org/play/celebritycalamity.html *The Complete Idiot's Guide to Money for Teens*, Susan Shelly *Prince Charming Isn't Coming: How Women Get Smart About Money*, Barbara Stanny Despite its title, *Buying a Car for Dummies* by Deanna Sclar is one of the better guides to introducing the dollar signs behind ownership.	*Buffett and Gates Go Bac. School* (2006) *The Motley Fool Investme. Guide for Teens: 8 Steps t Having More Money Than Your Parents Ever Dreame Of*, Tom and David Gardne

)w to exercise the epreneurial spirit	8. How to handle credit	9. How to use money to change the world.	10. How to be a citizen of the world
your kid to a confer- for entrepreneurs. your teen an email nding him that entre- eurs start nonprofits, ; in large companies, may be found on the of a church as well the world of science technology. kids who don't re to own their own ness need busi- skills. Encourage actor, musician, or ring designer to think mself or herself as a ntial entrepreneur. to fund a "start-up" ey can't do a summer Require a business	Don't cosign until you pro- vide credit card education and make expectations clear. Ask your teen to find out what a "teaser rate" is. Make sure that you charge interest when you loan money to your kids. It can be a low rate, but you want to remind them that borrowing costs money. Have your kid check her credit rating (if applicable).	Give your teen a subscrip- tion to *YES!* magazine. Ask your kid to list three causes that matter to her. Ask her to create a plan for supporting those causes. Ask your teen to identify and investigate which of the companies behind her favorite brands actually practices socially responsible business. Ask her to be specific about what makes them socially responsible. Microlending can engage kids in thoughts about giving critically in a place where they feel comfort- able: online.	This generation is more global than any past gen- eration. Once a quarter, give them their allowance in a different currency. Just as an exchange student would have to navigate the changes, have them calculate their purchasing power in the new currency. Then consider taking your teen to the currency exchange to change the currency into U.S. dollars.
ng My Virginity: How Survived, Had Fun, Made a Fortune Doing ness My Way, Richard son Jbu, Sit: How I t from Brooklyn to wood with the Same an, the Same Dog, a Lot Less Hair, Gary d Goldberg	AnnualCreditReport.com is the only official site for getting free credit reports. Ford's Wheel of Credit game introduces key terms and concepts: bit. ly/IMI _ FordCredit	Nonprofit organization dedicated to promoting ecological and social action: www.yesmagazine .org Engage empathy through Spent, an online poverty simulator: www.playspent .org http://mobilize.org www.kiva.org In 2010, Google hosted a Tech Talk on introducing the fundamentals of strategic philanthropy: http://bit.ly/IMI _ GooglePhilanthropy	*The Exchange Student Survival Kit*, Bettina Hansel Explore the world from your home: www .worldmapper.org is a collection of animated maps that highlight differ- ent types of cultural and geographic information.

When kids make financial

mistakes the operational question is not,

What did you do wrong?

It is, What have you learned?

The Ten Basic Money Skills

This is the stage of life during which you encourage kids to get behind the wheel of a car for the first time; in the same way, you should encourage teens to "test drive" good financial behavior by using tools such as budgets or engaging them in the realities of family financials. Now is the time to let them practice and apply in the real world while still benefitting from your watchful eye.

Basic Money Skill		
	1. How to save	**2. How to get paid what you're worth**
Actions: 16–18 Years	Introduce the concept of a credit union and give your child the option to join one. Send an email: "The quickest road to a good credit rating is a good savings record." Suggest that your child set a savings goal for a down payment on a house and calculate what she needs to save each month for the next ten years to attain it. Remind them that saving isn't just about money by going back to something you saved for a long time (such as your father's cuff links or your grandmother's wedding ring).	Ask your child to list three skills or talents he has and what he thinks is a fair fee for those skills. Have him compare his estimates to information he finds on the Web to see whether his are high or low. Introduce the concepts of equity, salary, wages, commission, and bonuses as ways of getting paid. Ask your teen which he thinks are the best forms of payment. Role-play the pay negotiation process with your kids before their next job interview.
Resources	*Think Single: The Woman's Guide to Financial Security at Every Stage of Life*, Janet Bodnar	*Free Agent Nation: The Future of Working for Yourself*, Sarah Pink A website for teens looking for a job: www.teens4hire.org

Financial competency is a way

for kids to manifest their character;

a way of playing out the essence of

who they are and who they will become.

Teens who exercise judgment about using money in thoughtful and competent ways are not just young people with a balanced checking account and a nest egg; they are young people who have made decisions about who they want to be and how they want to behave. Helping them use this stage to polish skills they've been working on over the years is one way to show your affection and respect for them.

Young people who have not learned to save, spend wisely, invest, handle debt and credit with self-awareness, and act philanthropically are more likely to have trouble leaving the nest, to accrue debt soon after high school, and to have chronic problems curbing the impulse to spend. These are the young adults who may spend a decade or more in a "delayed apprenticeship," trying hard to acquire financial skills, just when they most need them.

Personal Financial Safety Nets

By the time they become juniors and seniors in high school, it's time for teens to focus on how to develop and manage their own financial safety net. It's not necessary to scare them with visions of bag ladies and financial catastrophe to get their attention. But as they prepare for college or that first full-time job, they are both vulnerable to the larger world and a part of it.

Although legislation, including the CARD Act of 2009, improved the position of credit consumers, teenagers are still prey to the perils of poor financial choices. As they approach adulthood and more opportunity for trouble, they must be ever more capable of thinking critically about money.

Seventeen-year-old Ceara reports that a purchase at Gap or any of the shops targeting fashion conscious teens still elicits the automatic inquiry: do you want a Gap card? "I said no," she told me. "But he asked again, 'Are you *sure?*' and he was *big*!" Ceara wasn't suggesting the sales clerk threatened her, but she got the message that she was really supposed to consider the offer. She stuck to her guns and walked out of the store with her purchase and no extra debt.

Ceara knows how and why to turn down credit offers from her friendly retail chains. But what if she didn't understand that accepting "free credit" would cause a drop in her credit score that could follow her for years?

Economist Peter Passell maintains that "one of the most substantial changes in the U.S. economy over the last twenty years has been the shift of

In 2009, Congress passed landmark credit card reform. Here's what it means for your teens:

- Credit card issuers are no longer allowed to issue credit cards to those younger than twenty-one, unless the young person can get a cosigner or show proof of income.

- Credit card statements must clearly show the results of paying only the minimum payment.

- Credit card holders must opt in if they want to be able to go over the limit (and accrue the accompanying fees).

- Credit card issuers are limited in how they can change rates.

- Credit card issuers must give holders forty-five days' notice before changing anything.

- Credit card issuers can no longer raise interest rates if you default on another loan.

- Certain fees are now capped.

- Credit card issuers must apply payments to balances with the highest interest rate first.

financial risk from the institution to the individual. This means *if you cannot manage your own financial security you will be out of luck.* That is, financial safety nets must now be woven by each of us to some extent. As many parents have a hard time doing this for themselves, it's tough to pass along to kids."

But this lesson will be learned early among young people facing a tough job market as this book goes to press. College graduates in 2012 faced historic unemployment rates. And from St. Petersburg, Florida, to New York City to Palo Alto, California, teens find that high unemployment rates mean that laid-off adults and older people unable to retire are filling available jobs. Not only are kids under pressure to become financially self-sufficient by virtue of fiscal policy, but for many kids, this is happening when the job market is unwelcoming. Figuring out how to create a personal financial safety net is just basic economic self-defense.

No Operating Instructions Included

Today's parents are not less capable or caring than their parents and grandparents. The fact is that the issues of kids and money *really are* more complex and challenging than ever. Before easy credit, mass communication, and family mobility, financial values were communicated through the extended family. Companies have always aggressively targeted kids as consumers, but in the past they had fewer tools with which to do it. And parents did not have to compete in the same way with peers and media for their children's respect and attention. Breakfast and dinner at home were, to some extent at least, antidotes to the pressures of peers.

In the 1980s, attitudes and policies changed the financial landscape for parents and their kids. "Self-sufficiency" emerged as a value equated with virtue and discipline. It began with welfare reform and trickled up to the everyday experience of working-class and middle-class people. Prior to the 1980s, only a privileged few had easy access to the stock market, financial information, and financial products for saving and building wealth.

In the 1990s, the Internet and the rise of the "free-agent nation" fueled this growing regard for independence and self-management. The stock market and financial information became accessible online—and around the clock. Numerous financial products and services became available, making it more critical than ever that individuals be financially literate in order to make choices they had never been able to make before.

This shift of financial responsibility from institution to individual is, in a way, a true democratization of financial opportunity. But with this democracy comes greater personal responsibility. No longer can you let your retirement plans coast on autopilot while your employer (mis)manages your pension fund. You must choose between 401(k)s, IRAs, Roth IRAs, and a host of other financial options. And you may have the best advisors on the planet to guide you, but if you don't understand the basics of what they advise, they are essentially worthless to you. And explaining it all to your children can be like trying to teach a foreign language you've never spoken yourself.

As this new, more financially democratic—and complex—world has emerged, no one's been handing out operating instructions. Parents are left on their own to sort out their financial values and practices, much like trying to figure out those exasperating children's toys that used to come with four hundred pieces but no good diagram to help you put them together. In every part of a democratic society, *literacy matters*. To make a democracy—political or financial—effective, its members must know how to talk about, understand, and use the basic ideas and mechanisms of the culture.

Big Tasks for Stage Four

For this reason, the Big Tasks we discuss as part of each phase of development begin to take on greater consequence in Stage Four. These include

1. The Ten Basic Money Skills: real-world applications
2. Making mistakes and making recovery: the greatest gift you can give your kids is the opportunity to take risks and make mistakes while the stakes are still relatively low
3. Shifting from reliance on parents to reliance on self, including earning money, exploring entrepreneurship, and leveraging the power of regular, disciplined saving

1. The Ten Basic Money Skills: Real-World Applications

If teens are on track up to this point, they've been practicing the Ten Basic Money Skills in a low-risk, high-learning mode. (If you're just starting out, it's not the end of the world. You can still make serious progress.) Learning iteratively and cumulatively, they may well be sick of hearing about the Ten Basic Money Skills—but they will surely never forget them!

In this stage of financial apprenticeship, it's time to shift from practice to application, from the lab to the real world. As they go off on more trips with friends (without you as backup crew), prepare for college and life on their own, get their first car, fend for themselves in their first summer internship or part-time job, or take on more responsibility with family philanthropies or trust funds, they should now be dealing with real life and its consequences. The tasks and resources in this stage of the Life/Money Map raise the stakes for interaction with the larger world.

> **Common Teen Money Mistakes**
>
> The savings sinkhole
>
> The credit morass
>
> The collection obsession
>
> Overcommitment
>
> Lack of grace

2. Making Mistakes and Making Recovery

In a *New York Times* article about his life and career, Mark Levin, then chief executive of Millennium Pharmaceuticals, said, "One of the most important things I have learned is that failure is good for you. People who do great things in life are those who went through a lot of adversity. I've made huge mistakes along the way."

And tech entrepreneur Jan Davidson—who started a software company, David Associates (creators of MathBlaster and other top-notch educational software), with $6,000 and an Apple II computer and sold it ten years later for over a billion dollars—was famous for asking her staff each day about the mistakes they had made. "If you don't make at least ten mistakes a day," she would tell them, "you aren't learning enough."

Who among us has not failed to get comparative bids for a big-ticket item and regretted our impulsiveness later? Or who has not bought something without checking Angie's List or *Consumer Reports*, only to find we bought a lemon? And when the small print on contracts and credit agreements is so small, we can easily miss information that haunts us later.

The years between sixteen and eighteen are prime for great learning—and possibly the last low-stakes period in life for making great learning mistakes. Give teens the opportunity to take risks and make mistakes. When the mistakes show up, the operational question is not *What did you do wrong?* but *What have you learned?* Here are stories shared by teens (and one aunt) that offer pointed lessons.

The Savings Sinkhole

Eighteen-year-old Sam was ready to buy a car. He'd saved enough money to buy a used car, and his parents, wanting him to be responsible for the car from the start, encouraged him to find one and handle the purchase himself.

Sam looked up used car listings online and found a great buy, significantly less than the book price he'd expected to pay for the car he wanted. Thrilled at the savings he could demonstrate to his parents, Sam made contact with the seller, went to see the car, and learned it had been in a slight accident, which accounted for the low price. The seller seemed very up-front and told Sam a repair for the accident was estimated to be in the order of $150. Sam liked the car and felt the repair was within his budget—and still left him with a little money left over. So, without further consultation with his parents, he made the deal and took possession of the car.

Soon after, Sam took the car to a mechanic to get the repair made. To his chagrin, the mechanic informed him the repair would be extensive and would cost roughly ten times what the seller had estimated. Sam's eagerness (and good intention) to save money was undermined by his failure to do his homework *before* making a significant purchase. Similarly, had he checked in with his parents or looked up used-car-buying guidelines, they might have insisted he get the car inspected *first*.

His parents, hoping he would not forget this experience, advanced the money for the repair but insisted he pay them back over time. Wisely, they felt that bailing him out would allow him to forget the consequences of his action far sooner than he would by being reminded every time he made a payment to them.

Ironically, many kids absorb saving-money lessons eagerly. Being able to say, "But *Mom*, look at the money I saved!" seems like an easy way to gain approval while still getting what they want. The problem with this, as we all know, is that the advertising industry has become very clever about how they help people "save" money while spending it at the same time. Girls who shop exclusively at discount stores will say, "But Dad, I saved a couple of hundred dollars today," ignoring the reality of having spent $250 to do that. The moral of this story for parents is to be wary of focusing only on saving. If financial education is limited to an emphasis on saving at the expense of the other nine skills, kids will seek approval for saving while spending their way into a pile of debt.

Financial savvy at this stage consists of a balanced understanding of how each of the skills supports the others. If you're frustrated by your teen's spending habits, listen to how she talks about saving. If his savings account doesn't show real growth, if his checking account is not balanced, and if the word *budget* isn't part of his vocabulary, you may not be spending enough time on money messages that go beyond exhorting them to save.

In this case, Sam's parents showed strength in helping him learn from his savings adventure and expanding his notion of financial responsibility.

Perhaps the greatest gift you can give your kids is the opportunity to take risks and make mistakes. And when the mistakes show up, the operational question is not *What did you do wrong?* but *What have you learned?*

The Credit Morass

Seventeen-year-old Andrea received a credit card application in the mail. She had an active babysitting practice and cleared a few hundred dollars a month. She saved money regularly and thought of herself as pretty reliable. Because she was getting ready to go away for a summer program at a college in the next state, she talked her grandmother into cosigning for a credit card "for emergency purposes" (cosigning is now required for those under twenty-one—see page 120 for more about new credit card laws for minors). Because Andrea was usually very responsible, her grandmother agreed, with the proviso that Andrea would have to pay for anything that was not absolutely of an emergency nature and had to cover the balance each month.

Andrea's program schedule included several field trips each week. Away from home and in an environment of adventure, with new friends who seemed to have lots of money to spend, Andrea found many opportunities—and new "emergencies"—for using her new credit card. Within three weeks her balance was well over $400, and none of the charges could *really* be considered emergencies. By the end of the first month, she already knew she could not pay off the whole balance, so she paid just a part of it. She could, she reasoned, start to economize, and on average she would be in a better position to pay off the whole balance before the end of the next month.

But the next month brought more field trips, and the pressure to keep up with her friends as they ate, shopped, and enjoyed their outings meant that Andrea's balance kept growing—though her ability to pay didn't. By the time she returned home, Andrea's credit card was maxed out, and she was facing both interest fees and her grandmother's disappointment.

But Andrea's grandmother decided to grasp a teachable moment and gave her granddaughter a lesson in the art of restructuring debt. First, the grandmother paid off the credit card. Then she created a new "account" in which Andrea now owed her, instead of the credit card company. (She didn't cancel the card; she just put it aside for a while.)

Andrea had to sign a contract with her grandmother, agreeing to pay off the debt over a period of months. Andrea's grandmother lowered the interest rate from the 26 percent the credit card company was charging to 6 percent. It wasn't nearly what a real credit card would cost, but it did remind Andrea of the cost of credit. There was no charging available under the new contract with her grandmother. If Andrea wanted a new pair of jeans, she had to have the cash before making the purchase—and of course if she *did* have cash, it went to paying down debt first.

It took nine months before Andrea was free of debt. By then she was just a few months away from her first semester of college. Instead of forbidding her to have a credit card, her grandmother hoped she had learned her lesson about credit and how easy it is to get out of control. It worked: Andrea became a crusader among her friends, and the credit card became a real tool for emergencies, not a recreational vehicle. Andrea's new behavior arose from her grandmother's cool-headed commitment to helping her learn from her mistake rather than simply imposing punishment.

The Collection Obsession

Alex started to collect stamps when she was just a little girl and her mother's best friend gave her a plate block of beautiful stamps. As she grew older, she became entranced by the pictures and stories behind the stamps. And when she was twelve, she began to grasp their investment value as well. Relatives gave Alex stamps for birthdays and Chanukah, and part of her allowance went to buying stamps every week. As she got older, she attended fairs and shows where she traded for more stamps. By the time she was in high school, her collection was extensive and valuable.

For a long time, Alex's parents encouraged her passion for the stamps. How bad could this be? She was investing in a valuable collection and learning history, science, and geography at the same time. But by the time she was a junior in high school, her passion had become an obsession.

Alex spent more and more time studying stamps and more and more money on her collection. Finally, a stamp came on the market that was way beyond her resources, and she knew it was more than her parents could pay as well. But she wanted the stamp and was determined to get it by hook or by crook. She began to steal money from her parents. When she had enough money, she purchased the stamp and hid it in a notebook in her room. But getting the stamp did little to stem her hunger for the tiny works of art. She wanted more. She continued to steal and buy more stamps.

Eventually, of course, Alex was caught. Confronting her, Alex's parents gave her a tough choice: sell the collection to pay them back and gain some perspective or diversify her interests, selling part of her collection to pay them back and leaving the rest of the collection in safekeeping with them for a year. Alex was angry, but her parents did not back down. Finally, she chose option B and sold part of her collection to pay back her parents. The forced vacation from her passion gave her space to gain perspective.

Even though we normally applaud the emerging passions of young people, it's important to be aware when they spill over into less positive behaviors and need to be balanced or redirected. Alex wasn't a pathological thief, but she had become isolated from friends and other interests. Her passion had elicited so much approval throughout childhood that it was hard to give up. With the help of her family she has expanded her friendship circle and diversified her portfolio of interests—and she still has quite a valuable collection!

Overcommitted

At sixteen, Phil had a part-time job working for a company owned by one of his dad's best friends. Though he worked only twelve to fourteen hours a week, he was also president of his class, a once-a-week volunteer at the local humane society, and the center of attention among a great group of friends. He kept up his grades, though they were not as high as his parents thought they might be if he were not so busy.

Still, they felt he had a well-rounded life, and they trusted him to make good decisions about priorities. Phil's juggling act was precarious, but it worked reasonably well until his employer offered him a bonus to work on a special project that would last for three months and for which he could earn an extra $500 per month. He agreed, and the juggling act went into high gear. It wasn't long before Phil's mother noticed her son was dragging in the morning and irritable when he got home each night. His friends complained they didn't see him, so in an effort not to alienate them, he pushed himself to see them later in the evening. Not surprisingly, in the third month of this hectic schedule, Phil caught a cold—which turned into a serious infection that landed him in the hospital.

Phil's parents were proud of their son and pleased that he exhibited such a strong work ethic, but they realized he hadn't learned to set personal boundaries and that his desire to make money was not teaching him good habits so much as it was teaching him that doing it all required pushing beyond reasonable limits. Rather than issue an edict about what he could and couldn't do, the parents decided to work with him to set boundaries. His illness had forced Phil to pay attention, and his parents were able to use the insight that came of the crisis to help him think about how he wanted to live.

Neither Phil nor his parents wanted him to be less engaged with work, friends, or education—the question was how to manage his enthusiasms in a way that didn't undermine his health. Phil noticed that there was little room or time for himself in the schedule he had created. On his own, he decided to take at least half a day all to himself with no claims from the external world—and make sure he got enough sleep.

In the beginning this affected his bottom line, and the fact that his savings account was not growing as quickly as it used to troubled him. But as the months passed and his time-outs helped him grow stronger and more peaceful, Phil could see that being more purposeful about making money and spending time with others would probably pay off. By letting Phil make this discovery himself, his parents didn't make him feel less powerful; they just helped him gain needed perspective.

Forgetting Grace

Though it's not listed as one of the Ten Basic Money Skills, I've come to believe that gratitude should surely be addressed in that vein. The aunt who sent me the following email articulates a level of consternation that arises in the face of a disconnect between financial savvy and character.

She wrote: "I have four nephews and nieces, ages fourteen to eighteen, who live about two thousand miles from me, so I rarely see them at Christmas, though they know me well and we spend time together during the summer. Each year I spend time and money selecting gifts I think they will really like. And their parents (my siblings) tell me they *do*. But of the four, only my fifteen-year-old niece reliably sends a thank-you note. I'm tempted just to buy for her next year. Am I being unreasonable?"

The other three children in the family are making a big mistake with their aunt—and, patterns being what they are, they will likely repeat this mistake in areas where the stakes are even higher (a mentor who gives time or opens doors is not properly thanked and decides to stop providing support, or a client who is taken for granted decides to purchase services or products elsewhere) if an

---

Resources for Helping Kids Develop Grace

A Smart Girl's Guide to Manners, Nancy Holyoke

Tiffany's Table Manners for Teenagers, Walter Hoving

How Rude! The Teenagers' Guide to Good Manners, Proper Behavior, and Not Grossing People Out, Alex J. Packer, PhD

365 Manners Kids Should Know: Games, Activities, and Other Fun Ways to Help Children Learn Etiquette, Sheryl Eberly

Manners, by Kate Spade and Ruth A. Peltason

Dude, That's Rude! (Get Some Manners), Elizabeth Verdick

The Little Book of Etiquette, Dorothea Johnson

intervention is not made. If kids think they are *entitled* to presents, just because it's their birthday or a holiday of gift giving, they won't connect giving thanks with receiving gifts. In the mind of an entitled child, these are not *gifts* in the real sense of the word, but *loot*.

Short of cutting off the supply to make a point, what can the aunt do?

- Next year, her presents can be books that speak to the issue of gift giving and giving thanks. She might also give a donation to a nonprofit, in their name, with a letter about the importance of giving—and receiving—gracefully.
- When she sees them in the summer, she can initiate conversations about gift giving, including what giving and receiving symbolizes and how the exchange can be honored.
- To offer a slightly different perspective, she can suggest that next year they all exchange gifts they make rather than buy.
- She can speak to her sister or brother. One parent I know insists the kids write short thank-you notes as they unwrap gifts. One gift can't be unwrapped until the previous note is completed (and yes, he does allow email thanks). Though this approach is a little extreme, the point is certainly made.

Another option the aunt has is to use her time in the summer to be an etiquette mentor, not only on thank-you notes but also on the basics of using utensils properly at the table, introducing and being introduced, shaking hands, and the myriad other etiquette skills that are not routinely taught. When kids don't acquire these skills, it's usually because no one took time to teach them.

Why do I call gratitude and proper etiquette a money skill? Because at the heart of good financial relationships is a respect for reciprocity. When they learn the power of expressing appreciation for a job well done (labor well rewarded, a higher price for a beautifully crafted product) or respect for a fair exchange, young people develop healthier attitude about money in general.

The money mistakes chronicled here are committed and, for the most part, corrected by teens themselves. But key to each of the stories is the engagement of a parent or mentor who—without punishing, castigating, or shaming— helped guide the young person through a teachable moment associated with the mistake. As in any good learning experience, insight comes from the discourse, from the caring respect and involvement of a person who has the best interests of the teen at heart and acts on a profound conviction that the child wants to be a better person.

3. Shifting to Reliance on Self

The beauty of a conscious financial apprenticeship is that it provides a low-risk, sheltered environment for practicing the Ten Basic Money Skills. This stage is a launching pad for moving out of protective shelter into an arena of greater self-responsibility. Whether training for sports, a school play, or college entrance exams, a time comes when practice shifts to performance. So it is with one's financial apprenticeship. The most important Big Task for parents is to help children master the lessons of Stages One, Two, and Three. And essential to developing self-reliance and becoming self-sufficient is the ability to earn money, whether through employment or entrepreneurship.

Part-Time Work for Teens

First, the facts: Laws regulating employment of minors vary among states and U.S. territories. But according to the U.S. Department of Labor's Fair Labor Standards Act (FLSA), the minimum age for employment is fourteen. In addition, the FLSA prohibits the employment of minors in hazardous work (excavation, driving, and the operation of many types of power-driven equipment). There are, however, exceptions to FLSA restrictions. For example, minimum age requirements do not apply to minors employed by their parents or guardians. Young people of any age may also deliver newspapers; perform in radio, television, movie, or theatrical productions; and babysit or perform other minor duties around a private home.

The pressing question from parents is whether or not kids *should* work (presuming they have a choice, of course, as not all families have that luxury). The question has been studied exhaustively, and though the studies often conflict, there is evidence that the number of hours a high school student works each week is a significant factor in her academic performance and personal growth. That is, although working *more* than fifteen hours a week correlates with lower grades and impaired behavior, kids who work *less* than fifteen hours a week in school-based internships and job programs seem to acquire real benefits. Anecdotally, I can report that young people I encounter as interns, full-time employees, and even summer-camp attendees exhibit more sophisticated life skills and judgment if they have had some work experience in their formative years.

As with so much in child development, whether or not and how much your particular teen should work varies from family to family. But the value of early experiences in getting and keeping a job and managing earned money is great enough that, within a reasonable set of guidelines, I highly encourage teens to work—particularly during summer months. Here are some of the questions that you as a parent need to ask and the parameters you must put in place to ensure that work is a healthy choice for your child.

Will the work reduce the number of hours of sleep the teen gets? Teens really do need more sleep than we do. Adding responsibilities that significantly reduce teen sleeping hours is probably not a good idea. If the job is a priority, what other activities might be cut back to make sure that sleep isn't sacrificed?

Is it safe? Is transportation to and from the workplace convenient and safe? Do you know the company and have you met the employer? No self-respecting teenager wants Mom and Dad to show up at work like it's the first day of kindergarten, but as a parent you want to at least have an idea with whom your teen is spending time.

What's the cost of work and does it outweigh the benefits? If a uniform or particular style of dress is required that costs more than the child makes each week, help your kids make a cost/benefit analysis of whether this job makes sense.

Is the pay fair? Kids are often given "gofer" jobs that give them great work experience in exchange for relatively low pay—we used to call this "paying dues." But if it appears that a teen with exceptional skills (a young computer programmer, for example) or talent (great writing skills) or just incredible energy is being used excessively without proper compensation, you'll need to talk about what's fair and how to advocate for oneself with an employer.

Is your child meeting people, networking, or learning skills that will make a difference later in life? Keep in mind that there may be more to a job than meets the eye. I remember a few unbelievably tedious jobs I endured as a teen only because I wanted the paycheck enough to put up with the dull work. Only years later was I able to see just how terrific my employers had been and how much I had learned about the importance of reliability and discipline. In retrospect, I would not have given up those jobs for anything—but it might have been a hard call at the time! In fact, I once wrote a column on the value of a boring summer job, making the case that being imaginative enough to make more of that job than appears possible will give you an edge throughout your career.

Why this particular job? Is it his choice? Is it something you set up? Did he just fall into it easily? Although job-hopping is more acceptable now, you don't want to encourage too-frequent job changes. On the other hand, these are the years to experiment and try new things. Evaluate whether the job he's chosen is right for him.

Self-Employment and Entrepreneurship

Entrepreneurship is a powerful means of engaging kids in an exploration of money and business as well as an effective way to achieve independence, explore interdependence, and pursue deep interests. Although teen curiosity about entrepreneurship is high, in truth I am not terribly interested in having millions of kids start their own businesses. I want them to focus on their education. However, gaining the *skills* and *understanding* of entrepreneurship in this stage is valuable for a host of reasons:

- Whether or not teens ever start their own businesses, every employer seeks self-motivated, self-managing employees. Once shunned by many large corporations, the entrepreneurial employee is now in high demand.
- Lawyers, doctors, accountants, artists, writers, actors, consultants, and other professionals who function as sole practitioners discover quickly that a lack of business skills can undermine the pursuit of their chosen profession. As one teenage participant at Camp Start-Up, an entrepreneurship program offered by Independent Means, said to me, "I don't really want to have my own business; I want to be a lawyer. But eventually I may want to start my own practice." (Smart girl—she's planning ahead!)

Books to Inspire Emerging Entrepreneurs

Growing a Business, Paul Hawken

Body and Soul: Profits with Principles, Anita Roddick

Steve Jobs, Walter Isaacson

A Garlic Testament: Seasons on a Small New Mexico Farm, Stanley G. Crawford

Ben & Jerry's: The Inside Scoop, Fred "Chico" Lager

Losing My Virginity: How I've Survived, Had Fun, and Made a Fortune Doing Business My Way, Richard Branson

Our Wildest Dreams: Women Entrepreneurs Making Money, Having Fun, Doing Good, Joline Godfrey

- When job options are limited, young people will have an option (to be discussed in more detail in the next stage)—they can employ themselves.
- Exploring entrepreneurship is an excellent means of introducing the language and concepts of money into "real life." Balance sheets, profit and loss, budgeting—all these concepts may be understood more readily in the realm of "having my own business."
- Being able to add a self-initiated venture to the college application gives the applicant a competitive advantage.
- Finally, there's the relevance of introducing one of the most important paths to building wealth. A number of books (*The Millionaire Next Door* and *Rich Dad, Poor Dad* being among the more successful) have helped families understand how important it is to help kids see beyond the collection of a paycheck to the building of wealth over the long term.

Teaching teens about equity or company ownership, first through the concrete mechanism of a real company and later through investing in other companies, is one way to help teens see themselves as their own best security blanket. Although many families encourage kids to get an education and take a "secure job," in February of 2012, 12.8 million Americans were unemployed. Clearly, the next generation will need to pursue wealth building as a means of financial security, not just rely on paychecks from a so-called secure job.

In each stage of the financial apprenticeship I've encouraged the development of entrepreneurial skills, in part because it is a developmentally effective activity and in part because young people are often curious and intrigued by the notion. The success of Mark Zuckerberg, the young mogul behind Facebook, inspired many kids to experiment with building apps and offering services to make some money on their own. Every year, schools and colleges seem to add another business plan competition. Earth University in Costa Rica makes achieving a profit in your start-up a requisite of earning a degree. And the Theil Foundation encourages young people to drop out and start up! This provocative call to entrepreneurship is not for everyone, but it is a sign that making a job, not just taking a job, is a serious twenty-first century strategy to consider.

Not all first efforts are successful of course. The first-time entrepreneur is prone to making assumptions that cannot be supported; sometimes they simply don't do the math correctly.

I get very excited about mistakes made by young entrepreneurs. "This," I remind them, "is the best opportunity you will get to make big mistakes and have the stakes be so low. Making errors in your business plan when you are thirty or forty means there will be real consequences—from cash-flow problems to Chapter 11. But first ventures tend to be learning errors, not the end of the world."

So if you have a champion Girl Scout–cookie salesperson in your family, or a child who always has an idea for a business, help channel that wonderful energy right into a business plan—another exercise in financial skill building (see sidebar, Resources for Creating a Business Plan).

Resources for Creating a Business Plan

www.sba.gov/content/young-entrepreneurs

www.YoungBiz.com

The Young Entrepreneur's Edge, Jennifer Kushell

The Lemonade Stand: A Guide to Encouraging the Entrepreneur in Your Child, Emmanuel Modu

50 Great Businesses for Teens, Sarah L. Riehm

Self-Reliance and the Extended Family

Throughout this book I refer to parents and their kids. It should go without saying that financial education of the next generation is a collective responsibility all adults share. Whether you're a grandparent or close family friend, a godfather or an aunt, it is your obligation to help the kids in your life develop economic self-defense.

One night after I had given a talk to clients of an asset-management firm in Colorado, I was approached by a couple who explained, "We did a very poor job of raising our own children to be financially responsible. Now we see what terrible money habits they are instilling in their own children. We don't want to meddle in our children's lives, but we're terribly concerned about what will happen to our grandchildren."

I asked them to consider what they might do if, while visiting their grandchildren, they noticed that the kids had wandered into the road and their parents weren't taking any action about the behavior. Would they feel they were meddling to pull the kids out of the street and into safety? The couple immediately said, "Of course not."

Without *someone* intervening, children who miss the financial apprenticeship are vulnerable to the worst of life's surprises. Financial literacy is economic self-defense and we all have responsibility to function as money mentors, guides, and "consultants" to the next generation. When you perceive opportunities to reinforce a young person's inclination toward self-reliance, go ahead and take advantage of the moment. We each remember an adult (teacher, friend, special aunt or uncle) who made a difference in our lives. Do not be afraid to be that person for someone else. And if you are concerned you are playing the "buttinsky" in something that is the parents' business, ask them. Chances are they will welcome all the help they can get in raising financially fit kids.

Letting Go

This is the time to kick your money mentoring team into high gear as one way to help kids move beyond the safety of the family realm and into the sphere of the larger world.

In this stage, some of the work may be harder for parents than for the young apprentice. Letting go is a bittersweet challenge for parents. If the teen is eager and ready to break away, the parent may feel ambivalent about this young independent in their midst. Knowing that the very act of giving children skills for independence means they will need you less can feel like you are setting yourself up for a wrenching loss. On the other hand, if the child is wary of the world and seems to be avoiding independence, the family urge to protect may be at odds with the knowledge that life is not a rehearsal and that helping your child weave her own financial safety net is the most loving thing you can do.

Taking liberty with one of Robert Frost's great poems, we know that families are a place where, when you have to go there, they have to take you in. In a deep way, families are the most basic safety nets, and for many kids this can be tough to give up. And for parents in today's "sandwich generation"—facing the dual pressures of educating kids and caring for aging parents—it's especially imperative to help kids become self-reliant so there are sufficient resources available for the *whole* family.

These conflicting realities—the profound awareness that we live in a world that requires financial competency at an early age and the desire to keep kids close—mean that the work of this stage of apprenticeship may be as much the emotional work of parents as the skill-building and risk-taking efforts of their kids. Acknowledging this in some explicit way will make a significant difference in how the last stage of your teen's financial apprenticeship plays out.

If you can steer the arguments into conversations about what your teen wants his choices to add up to in life, you will feel more confident leaving the big decisions to him, trusting that he will make the right ones.

Rite of Passage: Independence Dinner

If you've been doing the pre-birthday dinners (as described on page 51), by the time teens are sixteen or seventeen you can use this annual rite of passage to focus on self-reliance and independence. Dressing up, going to a grown-up restaurant, and making it clear this is a night to talk about their growing independence will go a long way toward getting their attention. Talk about your individual roles in the process. Let them know they are loved and that encouraging independence is not abandonment, but a vote of confidence in their new capacities and abilities as maturing teens. Be sure to communicate your love and pride in their growing maturity. Give them a chance to describe their own feelings about independence.

If your teenager is not highly verbal or self-expressive and there is not a big response, don't worry. It's enough that you're getting the topic on the table—literally—and giving your teenager permission to have private fears and hopes. Suggest other ways to share thoughts and feelings about their fears and dreams for independence: writing, drawing, texting—whatever outlet they can use to share their expectations and worries about independence. Then share your own. Be explicit. If your expectation is for your teen to work summers now or live independently post-college, say so. If you expect her to earn money to pay for gas for her car, be clear about that. Parents often assume their children *know* what they expect. They're teens, not mind readers; if you want them to know something, you have to tell them, clearly.

The goal of this dinner is to mark a passage, to let teenagers know you are aware of the changes in their attitudes, their bodies, their lives. Let them know you understand that together you need to figure out a path to independence and self-reliance that is as mutually respectful and loving as you can make it. Launching a conversation about shifting from dependence on family to increasing self-reliance puts a topic on the table that you will both be able to revisit, discuss, think about, and experiment with over and over. Later, should tensions emerge because your daughter wants to go too fast (or slow) and you want her to slow down (or speed up) in the process, you will have a basis for talking together. You can say, "Remember the night we went to dinner and discussed how we each might have a different tolerance level for how fast or how slow this process is unfolding?" Or "Remember how we discussed ways we trigger the other's fears or anxieties about the process? It looks like that may be happening now. Let's talk about our feelings about dependence and self-reliance instead of yelling at each other about a specific event."

Whenever possible, move the conflict to a higher ground of discourse. When you are arguing about whether or not your daughter can go on an expensive ski trip with friends or airing your frustration that it is only the middle of the month and your son has already spent his allowance, it's important to remember that these conflicts may not be primarily about the money! You are likely arguing about matters of discipline, judgment, and values. If you can steer the arguments into conversations about what your teen wants his choices to add up to in his life, increasingly you will feel more comfortable leaving bigger decisions to him, trusting that he will make the right ones.

The Financial Expedition

Completing the fourth stage of the financial apprenticeship is a rite of passage, much like taking a driver's test or voting for the first time. In this section you will find six Financial Expeditions to help move the financial apprentice into full engagement with the world beyond the family. Think of these as Apprenticeship Final Exams—tasks that allow teens to demonstrate to you and to themselves that they have mastered the Ten Basic Money Skills and are truly ready to be on their own.

Invite your teen to elect one or more of the following projects to complete by the last year of the apprenticeship (ideally age eighteen, but this will vary). Ask for a plan and a timeline for executing the project—then hold them to it. Don't spring this task as a surprise; it's best to lay the groundwork early. Teenagers enter high school knowing they will have to take SATs. Let them know that senior year will include a Financial Expedition as well.

The Challenge: Demonstrate resourcefulness. Give teens a choice of tasks to be accomplished before high school graduation:

- Make dinner for six (invite friends if you need to) on $50—and no, a take-out dinner doesn't count. Delicious, nutritious, and fun are the criteria for success.
- Create birthday gifts for family members for under $10 each. The challenge is to use creativity to dazzle the recipient, not just come up with low-cost solutions.
- Take a friend to a movie, museum, concert, or some other event without paying for the friend's ticket (sneaking into the theater is not an option). This may require developing a deal with the theater or museum to get one free ticket in return for guaranteeing a certain minimum number of attendees. Or it may mean offering a special service that adds value and allows them to charge more for each ticket as a result, such as paying an extra $3.00 per ticket for a lecture about the place the kids are visiting.
- Raise $250 for a local charity. It should be a charity or cause of your teen's choice, of course. And whether it's running a 5K for a children's hospital or donating money to feed orphan horses, the act of raising the money must be their responsibility to achieve.

- Get an interview for a "dream" summer job or internship. You can remind your teen who is part of their social capital inventory, but you can't make the call for them.

The Challenge: Make a journey. As a family, select a vacation destination, then hand off the trip planning responsibility to your teenager. Make sure the plan includes a budget, transportation details, an itinerary, and a list of needed resources. Follow the plan and live the experience—mistakes and all!

The Challenge: Select an investment. Decide on a sum of money with your teen that he or she will have available to make an investment. (The amount will depend on your capacity and is less important than the action—a simulation can work here as well.) Ideally, this would be money drawn from a savings account, if that's a habit that has been underway since the teenager was a kid. The assignment includes selecting and researching a stock (or a mutual fund or index fund), then choosing a company or website through which the stock can be purchased. (Depending on your teen's age, you may need to execute the final purchase, but everything up to that point should be in her care.) Ask your teen to track the stock over time and let you know how it's doing. If she finds something else to invest in (a co-op, a social venture) and invests time instead of money, that's okay too.

The Challenge: Make a philanthropic contribution. With your teenager, decide on an amount from his or her savings account to make a donation to a local charity or cause. Ask for a report on the organization's cause, documentation of interviews with the group being donated to, and a plan for tracking the impact of the donation over time.

The Challenge: Make a difference. Ask your teen to design and complete a project that makes a positive contribution to the community: raising money for a particular cause or political campaign or organizing a group to offer community education on an issue that has gotten little attention. Successful completion of the assignment will include: (1) a description of the purpose of the project, (2) an organizational plan, (3) a list of resources needed and a plan for acquiring them, and (4) the intended outcomes.

Stress that making a difference can be as small as making an impact on one person. Changing the whole world is not required (though it's possible!); the purpose of the challenge is to be aware of what goes into making a commitment to make a difference. If you think the project may be bigger in scale than your teen can successfully accomplish, back off and let him make that discovery on his own—this is a learning project, not a no-fail project.

The Challenge: Execute a business venture. Challenge your teen to make money with a business venture. Whether it's organizing a car wash, setting up a babysitting service, or selling a product, the critical part of this project is to create a business plan and make a profit.

Moving On

If you've gotten this far in the apprenticeship journey, you've probably succeeded in providing a solid financial foundation for your teenagers. By now, I hope they are well on their way to mastery of the Ten Basic Money Skills (though that is a lifelong process!). But the journey has never been *just about the money*. To assess success, ask yourself this:

- Is my teen self-sufficient?
- Is he aware of spending patterns?
- Does she save regularly?
- Do I trust him to be financially responsible? Do I respect his growing independence?
- Does my family share financial values and do we walk our talk?
- Does my teen demonstrate integrity and good character in handling her financial life?
- In a life crisis (job loss, ill spouse, or divorce), will my teen have the financial acumen and resilience to cope with changed circumstances?

Kids who can and do learn how to pursue their dreams while managing the realities of money, and who are generous of heart with what they earn, become remarkable individuals. They are also safer in the world than peers who are financially oblivious. Raising financially fit kids is a challenging undertaking for all parents, but the results will last a lifetime—and beyond, as your kids teach their own kids sound financial values.

"Millenials are blessed, by age and the relative license to take risks that come with youth, and cursed, by lack of experience and an increasingly complex environment (they don't know what they don't know)."

—JOLINE GODFREY

Stage Five:
Ages 19+: Never Too Late

Today's young adult comes of age in a period that must at times feel like life in a human pinball machine. On the one hand is high global unemployment, unstable economies, and restructuring industries. Aggravated by overleveraged investment firms (Lehman Brothers), Ponzi schemes (Bernie Madoff), and reckless judgment (Jon Corzine), the last few years have ushered in the need for universal financial fluency for basic financial self-defense.

But the age of financial anxiety exists in parallel with the possibilities (good and bad) of disruptive change we can barely comprehend: space travel (Richard Branson's Virgin Galactic and Paul Allen's Space-Port are just two companies bringing science fiction to real life); organ regeneration and DNA mapping (now part of mainstream bio-tech funds); and the growing influence of artificial intelligence and robots.

The Life/Money Map
Stage Five/Ages 19+

Social/Emotional Development	Appropriate Money Skills to Master
Balances freedom with new responsibilities (apartment lease, first home, medical care, independent living, and so on)	Manages cash flow
	Designs and manages an annual financial plan
Finds long-term companions and love	Commits and executes on saving and investing goals; understands and contributes to a diverse investment portfolio
Begins to develop a strong sense of self and mastery in career or other endeavors	Is cognizant of civic responsibilities and obligations of paying taxes
Develops a social or moral conscience and/or a sense of faith or religious conviction	Applies money, time, or talent to philanthropic contribution
	Engages in financial conversations with a consideration of core values and productive outcomes
	Knows how to make a job, not just take a job
	Understands why and how to develop strong credit ratings

No one can ever be fully prepared for the unexpected, but the skills and knowledge recommended in Stage Five give young adults the capacity for being proactive in managing their lives, not just reactive to one crisis after another.

Coming of Age in a Tsunami Economy and an Era of Change and Exploration

Every generation has challenges, and it's the work of youth to meet those challenges. On the macro level, this generation will cope in the ways previous generations did—adapting, learning, changing, and leading. But on the micro level, in terms of your own individual offspring, the macro-economics of change are small comfort. What families want to know is this: how can we help our smart twenty-something channel his or her talents into leading a purposeful, independent, satisfying life *now*, while preparing him or her for a future we can hardly imagine?

Big Tasks for Stage Five

This chapter offers personal strategies for launching young adults, including three of the most crucial money skills for young adulthood:

1. Cash Flow Management
2. Savings and Investing
3. Entrepreneurship

These money skills are critical for people on the verge of launching themselves in life. To put this stage of life in context, let's take a brief look back.

Launch Americana

World War II caused a generation of boys to leave home en masse, returning as men with U.S. subsidies: the GI Bill, access to cheap mortgages, and savings from their soldier's pay. Many were courted to join a growing job market. These twenty-somethings returned to launch themselves into jobs and families with a national safety net and a welcome home from a grateful industrial nation that had roles for them (at least for the men; women who had enjoyed a brief moment of independence during the war years were expected to launch backward: either back into the home as a homemaker or back into jobs traditionally filled by women—jobs deemed unworthy of men).

By the late 1960s, images of flower children joining communes where they grew veggies and raised kids filtered into the national myth of how the next generation becomes independent. Then in the 1970s and 1980s, boomers tried every conceivable strategy for establishing independence, launching themselves into PhD programs, corporate careers, and movements (green, peace, energy, and so on) that offered supportive community.

By the 1990s, a growing economy and wealthier parents with resources and an inclination to indulge their children facilitated a slower, though still inevitable, transition into independence. For a small window of time, law firms, investment companies, a growing tech economy, and a voracious retail sector offered jobs that helped transport the next generation out of childhood and into the fast-moving, high-consuming world of "independence" and adulthood.

But as we make our way through the first quarter of a new century, young adults face the duality mentioned above: changing and interconnected world economies and unpredictable disruptions. And regardless of how educated, talented, or connected they may be, the next generation needs new skills and support to navigate this fast, connected, transforming world.

The Later Launch: What's Going On?

Families grapple with how to respond to adult children who are launching later and relying longer on parental subsidy. It's easy to forget that the pay phone, ubiquitous in the twentieth century and costing only twenty-five cents for a local call, has been displaced by smart phones and internet access that can cost well over $2,000 a year. ("How can I look for a job if I don't have a cell phone or laptop?" parents are asked.) The movie-and-a-burger date of the 1960s and 1970s has been replaced by concerts, clubs, hip eateries, and designer wear that is the base minimum for a night out. Transportation costs—including car payments, insurance premiums, and the cost of gas—have increased substantially, all while public transportation is being reduced in many areas.

Commentary on the social trade-offs of these new expectations could fill a different book. But to defuse the blame and frustration that can make family life fractious, let's look at some of the economic realities working against parents and their adult kids.

The Numbers: Unemployment, Underemployment, and Sprouting Kiosks

In September 2010, 60.8 percent of people twenty to twenty-four years old were employed. And those who have a job may not have enough of a job. According to a Gallup Poll in 2009, 31 percent of eighteen- to twenty-nine-year-olds were *underemployed* (employed but wanting to work more hours). They're twice as likely to be underemployed as fifty- to sixty-five-year-olds. Those who are underemployed are not only missing out financially, they're missing out socially, deprived of professional experience and the means to support themselves in truly independent lives.

With so many young people looking for jobs, many of those who do have jobs naturally are overqualified. In 2009, one in two college grads under twenty-five were in jobs that do not require college degrees. The Bureau of Labor Statistics calls this—working in a job beneath one's skill set—*mal-employment*. Although those with degrees in engineering, health, and other high-demand fields are still finding work (and may be in the vanguard of emerging industries), hundreds of thousands of others are finding themselves working as retail clerks, bartenders, and other jobs that don't demand the skills they've honed for four years. These workers earn 30 to 40 percent less than their fellow alumni in jobs that require college degrees, making them more likely to be dependent on parental support.

In fact, among those employed full- or part-time, more than a third (36 percent) of all Millennials (people born in the 1980s and 1990s) say they are dependent on financial support from their families, according to a 2009 Gallup Poll. Less than a third (31 percent) say they earn enough to lead the kind of lives they want, compared to 52 percent of thirty-six- to sixty-four-year-olds. A harsh economic environment and lack of preparedness are sending young adults back home to live off the kindness (or the grudging acceptance) of parents or grandparents.

Beyond the Numbers

Unemployment among young adults is not just a family concern; it's a national concern. What twenty-somethings face is not just the bad luck of graduating during a down cycle, but historic economic disjuncture.

Even as economic indicators signal slow growth, technology, efficiency, and productivity are replacing the learning and experience that come with an entry-level job in sectors where twenty-somethings traditionally got their start: service and retail. That electronic kiosk in the airport; the self-checkout machine at the grocery store; and the touchscreen waitperson at your local chain restaurant used to be entry-level jobs that taught discipline, responsibility, and character building through the bouts of drudgery that came with tedious work and dealing with hostile customers.

And it's not just low-level service or retail jobs. Law firms are automating paralegal-level work, hospitals use fewer technicians and more machines, manufacturing uses more robots and fewer people, utility workers are replaced by smart meters, meter maids by self-service parking meters—the list is seemingly endless and growing. High unemployment is not necessarily a sign that business is down—it's evidence that business is transforming. As a result of these gains to the bottom line, a generation is left without the structure and education of work to develop skills and identity—and an imperative to prepare for the all-too-present future.

Modern Prep

Young people whose entry into meaningful work is too long delayed may find themselves developmentally out of step in vital ways. Self-esteem and confidence comes from mastery of social situations, early accomplishments, and connection with friends and colleagues who open doors and provide leads. Unemployed twenty- to twenty-four-year-olds need new ways to prepare themselves for independence and self-reliance.

Of course, convincing a college grad that economic fluency is required to compete in today's economy does not always counterbalance their reluctance to put in the work and effort to learn and grow. Resistance is fueled by a fear of failure, of confronting past mistakes and bad habits, and of engaging in foreign territory—money and finances. As one mother said, "My college grad always has a reason this isn't a good time to talk, and when he listens, I know he is hearing 'blah, blah, blah.'" She speaks for many who despair that they can get a process started. And when mom and dad are ambivalent about letting their kids grow up, generational reluctance to let go and take off combine to slow the process down.

Dear Mom and Dad:

Change begins with you. The twenty-two-year-old who is able to finagle living expense money out of you may not feel good about it, but it's a lot easier than changing family patterns and embracing the responsibilities of adulthood. In other words, your young adult child may not be feeling a big incentive to make things different—thus the passive resistance, the pretend attention, and the avoidance.

You have to be the pattern changer. This is not the same as punishment. In Stage Two, I explained why the allowance is not a tool for behavior management. "The allowance is a way to practice money skills," I said. The same is true when they are twenty-two, twenty-four, and twenty-eight. These are your kids. You love them and want the best for them, and you hurt when they suffer. Changing financial patterns is about supporting growth, not punishing bad behavior.

Best, Joline

Modern prep for adulthood may require changing family patterns, but this is yeoman's duty. Three tactics can help:

1. Transparency: Tell them what you're thinking. Adult children are not mind readers and may not pick up signals, innuendos, or body language. You have to be clear: *"Sam, independence is an important quality in this family. I know you can't afford to live independently just yet, but we'd like to work on a plan with you to make this happen within the next nine months."*

   A timeframe is important; it makes things real. Nine months is the length of a school year and a natural gestation period. A year seems like "forever" away; nine months is a real deadline.

2. **Follow through and be prepared.** Before you sit down, prepare a simple chart illustrating what your son or daughter is currently spending (as far as you know) on food, subsidized housing, entertainment, and so on. Have receipts ready, pull up the bank account on the bank's website, and document *every* purchase or transaction, from a diet soda at the drugstore to the utility bill. Your job is to reveal the actual cost of real life on a regular basis. This is not the time to chastise or judge; it is an opportunity to notice what is real.

3. **The script.** Know what you want to say. An impatient, "We've had it! You can't go on like this!" will trigger defensiveness. Your job is to keep emotions low and set the stage for change. Read the case studies that follow and think about how they apply to your situation, what strategies or pieces of advice you can take away from them, and how you can develop a dialogue, not just a *monologue* with you doing all the talking.

Flip Open

3. How to spend wisely	4. How to talk about money	5. How to live on a budget	6. How to invest
Have twenty-somethings considering buying a car figure out the total costs, including financing and average cost of repairs, for a new, slightly used, and "almost classic" auto. Challenge them to put their entertainment on a budget and to look for at least two free entertainment opportunities each week, such as free concerts or free art openings.	If you haven't already, have "The [other] Talk"—the one about prenuptial agreements, preferably before she brings home Mr. Right. Don't shy away from discussions about how difficult or easy one generation had it over another. Look up labor statistics and other real facts to cut through the rhetoric.	Require a multiyear budget that accounts for what they'll need (tuition, rent, food, etc.) including the amount you're going to contribute. Introduce them to Mint.com, or another digital budgeting tool.	Tap into the innate desire t see change with investing studying more about "impa investing," which consider the social and environment impacts of the investment. Match goals with types of investments, such as havi safety net with low-risk bo
Use the automotive resources at edmunds.com. Find interesting and quirky ideas for life on a budget at lifehacker.com.	*I Do, You Do . . . But Just Sign Here*, Scott N. Weston and Robert J. Nachshin The U.S. Department of Labor Bureau of Labor Statistics: www.bls.gov	Find cost-of-living comparison tools and other resources at bankrate.com.	*The Wall Street Journal Complete Personal Finance Guidebook*, Jeff P. Opdyke *Impact Investing*, Antony Bugg-Levine and Jed Emers

w to exercise the ≡preneurial spirit	8. How to handle credit	9. How to use money to change the world	10. How to be a citizen of the world
≡preneurs take risks, ≡ding the risk of work-≡r free as a volunteer, ≡ee, or apprentice to ≡intellectual capital. b is "beneath" ≡trepreneur—dog ≡ng, car washing, and ≡ing are all legitimate ≡res, even for the Ivy ≡ue student (or grad).	Be sure to talk about student loan debt. Even if they're fortunate enough not to need it, it's all around them. Connect credit to indepen-dence. Remind them that if they use credit poorly now, it will make it harder to find a place of their own later.	Invite young adults to be a part of your family's giving decisions. Twenty-somethings want to know their time and money is being used well. Talk about how you assess the effectiveness of your donations and ask for their ideas on how they can improve your process.	Have a friend who does business in China? Know someone in Costa Rican real estate? Set up lunches or meetings with your peers to give your kids an opportunity to expand their horizons.
≡100 Startup, ≡ Guillebeau	Get a free credit report annually, without obliga-tion, at annualcreditreport .com. Compare credit card rates, benefits, and features at creditdonkey.com.	Guidestar.com rates most philanthropies' effective-ness based on government filings. Calvert Social Investment Foundation created a tool to measure the impact of donations by quantity, term, geographic area, and sector.	Young people interested in how the government helps in global challenges should check out U.S. Aid, the federal foreign assistance program: www.usaid.gov. Kahn Academy has hundreds of great teaching videos, including a twelve-minute introduction to currency exchange:bit.ly/ IMI _ Kahn _ Currency.

Every generation has challenges,

and it's the work of youth

to meet those challenges.

The Ten Basic Money Skills

The Money Skills do not become obsolete as soon as young adults gain their financial independence. Just as with physical fitness, financial fitness must be practiced and continually developed in order to be effective.

Basic Money Skill		
	1. How to save	2. How to get paid what you're worth
Actions: 19+	If you're still giving an allowance, enforce saving messages by giving allowance in three- or six-month CDs. They'll need to hold on to it—or get a hard lesson in tapping into an investment too soon. If they don't already have one, help them set up an IRA or Roth IRA. They'll thank you later.	Encourage doing research to find out the average salaries for entry-level jobs in different industries and in different parts of the country. Set up practice interviews with your colleagues before they do the real thing. Shyness is a condition, not an excuse. Suggest using alumni officers, former scout leaders, teachers, camp counselors, coaches, and music instructors to acquire relevant introductions to anyone with whom they might share a meaningful connection. Personal recommendations, not resumes, are the most effective path to the next great professional experience.
Resources	*Get a Financial Life*, Beth Kobliner *How to Be Richer, Smarter, and Better Looking Than Your Parents*, Zac Bissonnette	*The Adventures of Johnny Bunko: The Last Career Guide You'll Ever Need*, Daniel H. Pink and Rob Ten Pas

Give young adults the capacity

for being proactive in managing

their lives, not just reactive

to one crisis after another.

Case Study One: Dave graduated from college in June. Six months later, he's depressed, looks for work sporadically, and hangs out with friends in between temp jobs. You give him $100/week to help him get around and cover phone and computer charges for the job hunt. His search process seems desultory at best.
Script:

Parent: Hey Dave, your energy level seems pretty low. Is the job hunt getting you down?

Dave: Oh no, I'm sure something will come up soon. It's all good; no problem.

Parent: Well, your mom and I think we've not been giving you the kind of help that might make a difference, so we want to try a new plan. We'd like you to sit with the two of us tonight to go over a few ideas.

Dave is uneasy but he can't really say no to the meeting. Later that evening . . .

Parent: Dave, we've been giving you money to get by for the last few months, but it's not enough to manage in a meaningful way, and it must make you feel like a little kid to still be getting handouts from your parents. We'd like to help you get on a path to greater independence. Any ideas how we might do that?

Dave: Well, as soon as I get a job, I'll be fine—this is okay for now.

Parent: Well actually, it's not working for us. We're awfully proud of you and know what you can do. You've mastered all the big challenges that came your way—from learning to tie your shoes to playing soccer as a champion. Now we want to help you master independence. We'll begin by giving you a larger lump sum once a month that you can manage for the whole month. At first we'll sit down weekly to go over your cash flow plans, but as you get the hang of it, we'll meet every two weeks, and then once a month.

Dave: So how is that going to help me get a job?

Parent: It won't magically get you a job, but while we're reviewing income and expenses, we'll also talk about projects and work you can take on in the next few months that will help you get the experience you need to get a job. For example, your mom knows someone who might be able to get you an internship at the radio station in town, and I have a buddy who is looking for someone to manage a project for him. It's short term, but it will help build your resume.

Dave: I appreciate the help, Dad, but really, I'm doing fine—no big deal.

Parent: I hear you Dave, but you didn't hear me. Independence is something we value in this family. And just as we set goals for other parts of our lives—such as watching my weight, helping the church get a new roof, and adding sales at my business—your independence is a goal we share as a family. We need to set the goal, make plans, and stick to it with actions and follow-up that help you achieve that independence. I know it's not easy, but you aren't alone; we're your wingmen in this process!

Dave: Does this mean you're kicking me out?

Parent: It means we're tracking how well we all do in getting you into the next phase of your life.

Over the next three months Dave and his dad meet regularly, not missing any meetings. By the end of month two, they are still meeting monthly, but Dave has a clear idea of his expenses and is managing the monthly allowance—and not asking his dad for money like a five-year-old. Dave has had a few good work experiences and is now planning to take an environmental services degree at the local community college. He doesn't ask his dad for handouts any more. Though there is still a subsidy, it is less than it was six months ago, and the plan is to reduce it again in three months.

Case Study Two: Mary Ann graduated from a top school with honors. In spite of a great resume and good recommendations, she isn't making headway in her chosen field. She had a couple of offers but felt the salary didn't recognize her experience. She graduated ten months ago and soon will be competing with a new batch of college grads. She's been rooming with a friend and lately has had to borrow money from her parents to meet her share of the rent.

Script:

Parent: Mary Ann, this is the third time you've had to borrow money for rent. I know you don't want to move back home, and we want to support your ability to be independent, but this plan isn't working for any of us. We'd like to schedule a brainstorming session with you later this week. Come for dinner and let's explore how we can get you on a plan you can manage.

Mary Ann is suspicious, wondering what they are going to spring on her. She wonders if they're going to make her move back home, but it's also a free meal. She shows up for dinner.

Parent: Mary Ann, we know the job offers you've had are not quite what you expected when you graduated, but you're not gaining experience of any kind, and the lack of income is putting your independence at risk.

Mary Ann: You know that if I take a lesser job, I risk not getting a job in my profession! I worked too hard to turn away from the field now! Just a few more months, and I'll be fine.

Parent: We're happy to make that part of a plan, but we need a bigger, more comprehensive plan—not just because we don't think it's appropriate to be subsidizing this level of lifestyle when you aren't working, but because we know how capable and ready for independence you are. Can you suggest a more definitive plan?

At this point the parents have put the responsibility back on Mary Ann for a plan. She knows that either she comes up with a plan they will support, or any plan they devise may not be one she wants to live with. Mary Ann counters.

Mary Ann: Okay, if you'll pay my rent for another six months and I *still* don't have a job, I'll take something else then.

Parent: That's more generous than we had in mind, but we'll offer this: we'll give you a lump sum amount that will cover your rent for the next four months, plus a little more to cover your gas, bills, and food. You will need to manage that money. If you can make it last longer than four months, then you have longer to hold out for a job in your field; if you keep your current lifestyle and don't cut back, you'll need to find a job sooner. But managing cash flow is not easy, and we don't want to increase your anxiety unnecessarily. During this time, I'll meet with you once a week to work together to review cash flow and how you're managing your budget. Once you get the hang of it, we'll meet every two or three weeks. But this way, you'll gain a little more time to search—and develop financial skills you'll need when you have a salary of your own.

The lump sum solution was one that Mary Ann did not see coming—getting greater responsibility for managing her life, before she has a full-time job, was a surprise. But she accepted the offer and met with her parents regularly. That dream job still had not come through at the end of five months (she had managed to eke out another month by carefully managing her cash flow). Her parents agreed to continue subsidizing her expenses for another three months beyond the original deadline, but only at about one quarter of what she had been getting. This was enough to convince her that an interim job was a good idea.

Consistency and support are key to helping young adults take charge of their destiny. As long as you are caretaking, they don't have to. It's not about whether you can afford to subsidize them; it's about helping them become self-reliant.

Case Study Three: Three months before his college graduation, Jack's grandfather died, leaving him a small trust fund. In a letter Jack received at the reading of the will, his grandfather encouraged him to "use the money well: invest it, start a business, and pursue something you care about."

Jack hasn't quite found himself, so he used part of his trust fund to try a few things out: he bought a classic car with the intention of refurbishing it and selling it to make money. He underestimated the cost of the work and lost money on the car. Then he decided to go into business with a friend. Unfortunately the friend drank more than he worked, and once again, Jack lost his investment. He's still living at home and is investigating the possibility of buying a franchise. Thanks to his parents, his living expenses are minimal, but the trust fund is diminished. His dad is concerned that Jack is too cavalier about his inheritance.

Script:

Parent: Jack, I heard you mention that you're down to about half of what your grandfather left you in his will. I know he encouraged you to do something that mattered, but I suspect he didn't think you'd go through it so fast. Would you like some help in planning how to steward what you still have?

Jack: Thanks, Dad, but I'm pretty sure this deal I'm working on is a "go," and I'll earn that money back in no time.

Parent: Maybe so, Jack, but your grandfather raised me to be a pretty good steward, and I'd be breaking my promise to him if I didn't help you become a good steward, too. You still have some money left, in part because you're living here rent free and we're still subsidizing your lifestyle. It's easy to see that money as "play money," but it was meant to give you a meaningful start in life.

Your mother and I love you—we like having you around—so we've been happy to have you live here. But unless you take a little coaching about how to steward your inheritance, we'll need to rethink the way we help you—I don't want to help you be too carefree about the gift your grandfather left behind.

Jack: What do you mean? Are you telling me what to do with my money? Grandfather left it to me to do what I want.

Parent: That's partly true, Jack. But he also wanted you to use the money well. In this family, our values about how to steward money are pretty clear: we do due diligence, we seek expert counsel for big decisions, and we think about how to manage capital in such a way that we can make it grow, not just spend it down. I know if your grandfather were still alive, you would be talking with him about how to manage this money—he loved coaching you. You might even have done some coinvesting with him.

But since he's not, here's my thinking. You need a coach or a mentor for what's left of the inheritance. I'm happy to be that coach, but we can identify someone else if you'd prefer—maybe Aunt Jane would work with you. She's run her own business pretty well. I'm happy to have you continue to live here rent free for a few more months, but only if you get the kind of advice and support to become a good steward that we should have helped you get earlier.

Giving young adults access to significant funds without corollary instruction is like giving an inexperienced driver a race car with no instruction: it's dangerous and unfair to the driver. When our children don't know what they don't know in economic terms, our responsibility is to make sure they get the knowledge they need—to drive the car safely or to manage the money wisely. It's hard for young people—really, all people—to acknowledge the need for help. But giving them choices that let them ask for help is a strategy that helps them preserve their dignity while acquiring skills they need now.

In each of these cases, the parents communicated their personal discomfort, shared the values of the family, and offered measureable action plans. The younger generation may not share or adopt your values, but as long as they are accepting your subsidy, respecting *your* values is not an unreasonable expectation.

Money Skills for Adult Responsibilities

As I said at the beginning of the chapter, each of the Ten Basic Money Skills is important, but three are high priorities for young adults.

I. Cash Flow Management

Doling out money, a bit at a time or in response to intermittent need, does little to develop skills for navigating complex economic lives. Subsidizing adult children undermines and slows down their ability to develop skills and live their values in a demonstrable way. Cash flow management—whether for one's personal budget, a business idea, or the care and nurturing of something they are personally responsible for (such as an apartment, a pet, a car, a child)—is a skill that, when mastered, tells employers, partners, friends, colleagues, and trustees that they can be trusted. It also projects character and values in a way that few other adult acts can. Please note: I am not suggesting that a failure to sustain financial responsibility is proof of lack of character. Life is messy and not entirely within our control—this is clearly demonstrated by such events as illness; the disruption of work and life that comes with natural disasters such as earthquakes, floods, and hurricanes; and economic effects that are outside of people's personal control. I simply mean that when a person masters cash flow management, it is a powerful way to garner the respect and trust of others— which is perhaps most needed just *when* those acts of God or bad luck appear!

The hard work facing parents is to decide that *the dole is out; managed subsidy is in*. If you are quietly forking out money each month, whether in rent checks or cash for gas, and you and your child do not have a clear and explicit mutual plan, you are undermining the next generation's independence, no matter how well intended your actions. We develop the discipline of cash flow management by managing cash flow.

FACING THE NUMBERS

Cash flow management is just a plan for anticipated cash expenditures for a twelve-month period as illustrated in the table that follows. But skilled cash flow management takes practice, lots of it. Kids who have practiced with an allowance since they were twelve will have had plenty of time to get proficient. Adults need to be dogged to master the skill and discipline of managing cash flow.

	Jan	Feb	Mar	Apr	May	June	July	Aug	Sept	Oct	Nov	Dec
Fixed expenses												
Rent												
Transportation												
Food												
Insurance (health, auto)												
Tech (phone, computer, and so on)												
Variable expenses												
Ski Trip												
Dates												
Clothing												
Medical												
Birthday, holiday, and wedding gifts												
New skis												
Emergency/ catastrophe												
Caught in a coup while traveling												
Food poisoning in Mexico, have to be airlifted home												
Arrested at Occupy Wall Street, need bail money												

To begin, fill out the form together, embracing real life and not some hazy version of what you think (or dream) is happening. If he's charging iTunes and Amazon purchases on your credit card, include that. If she gets a manicure a few times a month, add that in. We begin with what is, not what we'd like it to be. This is called *transparency*. It is a clean chance to face the numbers and examine lifestyle assumptions reflected in the monthly detail of expenses and income.

The use of a twelve-month chart also helps demonstrate how variable cash flow is. They have three friends getting married next June? Project the cost of gifts, clothing, and travel to the wedding. They've come to expect a ski trip in March? Estimate how much cash they will need in March. People don't appreciate the need to attend to the flow of income (and savings) until they grasp the rhythms of how they spend their money.

Just as recording your caloric consumption means counting *every* calorie in order to capture your real intake (including those calories that starkly document your weakness for ice cream) to prepare for achieving physical fitness, good cash flow management means counting *every* cent to prepare for achieving financial fitness. Although chances are that the annual cost of your twenty-something is higher than anyone wants to know, accounting for that cost is critical to financial fluency: knowing what is actually happening in their financial lives.

And whether you worry that you're tapping your own pension fund to subsidize your kids or you can well afford the cash, the scale may be staggering if it hasn't been tallied before. (Note to parents: yes, your advisor or bookkeeper *could* do this task. It is way more impressive when done live, with parent and adult child in the room!) When you have finished, just let the news soak in: this is what's real.

CASH FLOW MANAGEMENT PLAN: INCOME

One of the great benefits of family is the safety net. Even in the most precarious families, there is a sense that our basic needs will be met, somehow, or that the difficulty will be spread and managed together. Involving a twenty-something in the process of covering and managing cash flow expenses is one way to prevent the safety net that every child deserves from turning into the cocoon that keeps her from realizing her best self, while helping her see her place in the family support group. Understanding the disconnect between her belief in her independence and self-sufficiency and her actual role as the biggest sponge of family resources can help focus and adjust attitudes.

Once the costs of the young adult's lifestyle are clear, we turn to income—how the cost of the lifestyle will be covered. Young adults rely on three major sources of income—subsidy, earnings, and windfall—all of which can be managed effectively and sensibly.

Subsidy. Whether you're doing their laundry or paying cable bills, you're subsidizing. Label it and be clear about what you are willing to underwrite and for how long. Kids will make plans for themselves when they have real information. If you say: *"You can live at home for X months; I'll pay your car insurance, and I can subsidize your living needs up to $150 {or $500 or $2,500, whatever your number is} for a year while you get yourself settled. But on {fill in the date}, I expect you to be self-supporting or to give me a plan that shows how you are getting there."*

Obviously, parents who subsidize kids in the early years of independence are demonstrating love and support. But subsidy without guidelines undermines the young adult's ability to develop muscles for self-reliance. And if they don't develop those qualities themselves, it will be hard for them to model them for their own kids. Do you want to be subsidizing grandkids, too? Choose what you are able to subsidize, name it, provide, and then stop when you say you will.

Earnings. If they were earning at an adequate level, presumably you'd not need this chapter, right? But just because they're not earning a six-figure salary is no reason not to factor earnings into the cash flow equation. If they work Saturdays and make $100 a week, that's not just "spending money." It's money that is counted as income, along with the amount you subsidize. Earnings can come from paid work, projects, residuals, and even trust distributions. An expectation of earnings to supplement your subsidy is a way to keep the next generation focused on their goal: independence. As their earnings increase, your subsidy should decrease. Really.

Adolescents sometimes resist the institution of a fixed allowance because they intuit that their parents will expect accountability. Twenty-somethings may resist factoring in their earnings for similar reasons. However, over time and as their contribution grows, they feel pride and accomplishment. Make sure earnings are noted in the cash flow plan, no matter how small or intermittent.

Trust income, or investment income, is another form of earnings, and we include it here because kids with trust funds or income from investments can be as oblivious to cash flow as kids who are fully subsidized by parents. In both cases, opportunities to develop financial fluency are lost.

You don't have to envision the 1 percent to think about trust income. Families that set up any college savings fund may be tapping that fund to pay for education-related expenses. In the interest of transparency, include that income in the cash flow plan. But for kids who do have substantial distributions and still experience a chronic gap between income and expenses (covered by parents or by dipping into principle), the problem is likely not just that of the young adult, but of the system in which he or she is operating.

So how should the trust fund distribution be handled? If the money is "theirs," what's a parent to do? Young people who overspend trust distributions may not be making terrible decisions. If they've chosen to make an investment in a piece of land or a growing stock, for example, or if they've made a contribution to a cause they feel strongly about, the individual decision may be a good one.

However, if it's not made in the context of a sustainable cash flow plan, if they are not developing the rigor to make judgments within a larger financial vision, they are not gaining experience they will need for the long term. And when families fill the gap between a substantial distribution and expenses with subsidies, however intermittent, they rob the young adult of the chance to acquire skills for a more sophisticated approach to managing assets and income. The role of parents and trustees is to help the beneficiary make good decisions. This may be the time to call in trustees as part of your new mentoring team.

Windfalls. Include the tax refund from last year's summer job or the cash in the birthday card from Aunt Susan. Also include the winnings from that random lottery or the online poker game (and of course the losses must be noted as well!). Young people often think of windfalls as "free cash" that doesn't have to be managed and is disposable for iPads, ski trips, and other lifestyle expenditures. It's targeted to a specific act of consumption, as opposed to being factored into the cash flow plan. But windfalls are income (like a paycheck or subsidy) and should be recorded and managed as such. Again, it's about *transparency* and *reality*. If a ski trip as an expense is noted in the cash flow expense column, and the windfall from Aunt Susan is classified as income—and it balances out— then it's part of the plan.

But the tax refund or the birthday cash labeled "untouchable" is adolescent "mad money," not subject to the sober financial plan of a young adult. Money kept outside the realm of one's cash flow plan has a magical quality (remember the tooth fairy?). The Stage Five adult's job is to focus on what's real, developing skills to manage assets in the context of a bigger vision, for the long term.

2. Saving and Investing

If cash flow management is a reality check, investing is a strategy for making conscious choices, including that of setting aside assets to use in the future: to make a difference with philanthropy, to realize a vision, to support a family, to start a company. Investing is a means of shifting from reliance on the parental safety net to creating one's own safety net.

After the economic collapse in 2008, interest rates became so low as to make the act of saving seem like an act of folly. But as economist Peter Passell reminds us, "We all have to save, and expected returns on medium-risk investments are probably decent looking twenty to thirty years out." This is the moment when young adults get the greatest advantage of time. If you gave young Max or Molly shares of Apple or Google when they were twelve, investing may be familiar now. But if all they did was watch the stock go up and down as spectators, they are likely still not feeling confident about what it means to invest in a more serious fashion.

GETTING STARTED

This is not a chapter on how to invest. This is the chapter on how to get them ready to read that book on investing. Just as banks and credit card agencies target teens with their most aggressive marketing tactics, college students and young adults are prime targets for investment institutions—not because young people have a lot to invest yet, but because relationships forged early with financial advisors and bankers can evolve into fee-producing relationships that last for decades.

Young people who have successfully navigated the previous four stages of the Ten Basic Money Skills already understand how to do due diligence. They have likely had sufficient practice in the creation of a portfolio, and they understand many of the bigger questions that confront the new investor.

But imagine you're visiting Turkey and get separated from your tour group. Up to this point, you've been fully reliant on your guide and translator to help you understand where you are and what you are seeing. Suddenly you're on your own, without the language you need to find your group. Without some basic level of fluency, you are just a vulnerable stranger in an exotic city. This is the situation that unprepared twenty-somethings face as they consider how to invest for the future. Fluency is key to success in the choices and decisions they will need to make.

AN IMMERSION COURSE IN INVESTMENT FLUENCY

For the twenty-something, there is nothing new that he or she needs that can't be gained by a review of the tasks in Stage Four. At any age we need to understand the language of investing—literally, the vocabulary; the process of due diligence, or doing one's homework on people and opportunities; and the numbers, or what constitutes a true return on investment—for example, what percentage of our investment is going to pay fees and how long a return on investment will take.

I am reminded of Sam, a client who was intent that his adult children develop a measure of economic self-defense. In the beginning, Sam was concerned that his adult children would resist his desire for them to become more financially sophisticated, and indeed, they were leery of their father's plans. But everyone agreed to try. Sam was thoughtful about how to make the learning process engaging and meaningful. It's is easy to replicate, and I share it here:

1. Setting the stage. Sam didn't say to his kids, "I don't trust your financial skills, so you have to come for remedial financial education classes." He said, "We have a great family, and I'd like to help us all continue to grow and be great. I'm going to create a regular Family Council where we learn together and improve our skills together, and I hope you will participate."

2. Creating a learning climate. Sam decided that each of the family council meetings should offer time to share activities they had loved together since the children were young. Half the day was devoted to building financial skills; other parts of the day were open to enjoying one another's company in outdoor activities. And when they met to learn, the environment chosen was comfortable—sometimes an outdoor patio, sometimes a lake house,

and sometimes a big comfortable living room. Windowless classrooms were banned!

3. **Establishing process.** Sam made it clear that this was a long-term commitment. He let his adult children and their spouses know that the journey they were beginning was more like learning to play tennis, requiring practice and time, rather than getting a one-time workshop on backswings. He asked for a commitment to a year of work through a curriculum for financial fluency. Then they would evaluate how the process was going.

4. **Building relevance.** The first session began with a review of articles in the *Wall Street Journal* and *Vanity Fair* and the fashion pages of the *New York Times*. Sam wanted his kids to approach their sessions by understanding how investing connected to their daily lives: they discussed the oil spill in the Gulf, the failure of a major fashion house, and the effect the 2011 tsunami in Japan would have on some family investments. In other words, Sam made the process relevant to the values, choices, and real financial interests of the family.

5. **Practice.** Four sessions into the process the group decided to start an investment club to apply some of what they were learning. There are many ways to practice; the club was just one. The important thing was that now they had explored basic investing policy; they understood how to do at least preliminary due diligence. They had vetted good advisors and experts to consult on some of their decisions. In short, they were ready to be responsible investors.

Sam's process is not perfect and won't fit every family. But it's a model that families can adapt to their own situation.

HEDGE FUNDS, DAY TRADING, AND MUTUAL FUNDS

By now it should be clear I'm talking about how to prepare young adults to be thoughtful, lifelong investors. For some, this will lead to relationships with financial advisors and hedge fund managers. Others will be emboldened to try their hand at managing their own investments. And some will decide to trade modest returns for time to pursue other interests by making regular deposits into one or more mutual or index funds. When young adults have a frame of reference for understanding what it means to invest, their choices will be informed decisions, not just wild stabs in the dark.

Investing has evolved in a bifurcated way. On the one hand are investors with modest assets who find it hard to identify advisors who will give them real face-to-face time to consider good investment strategies. Increasingly there are minimums for talking to a live advisor, and many young adults do not have the assets to qualify for the minimum.

On the other hand, at the higher end of the asset spectrum, young people may have easy access to the most sophisticated investment advisors but not have the knowledge and experience to know whether they are being given good advice. In both cases, teaching the basics of investing is economic self-defense for the family. Like wearing seat belts, it's just a good practice for life.

PRACTICE INVESTING AND EXPERIENTIAL LEARNING

We learn by reading, watching, listening, trying something out, remembering the consequences of our actions, and trying again. Tactics for helping the financial novice develop investing fluency include

- Time. Arrange four to six meetings with your adult children in an eighteen-month time period. They will have time and opportunity to become familiar with the financial vocabulary (or at least a lot of it), read stories that demonstrate a variety of investing experiences, and have both simulated and real investing experiences.

- Constancy. Parents say, "My son/daughter is *so* busy, there's just no time for this." This usually means that one or both parties are not yet serious about the process. When you get a toothache, you'll clear the deck to get to the dentist and deal with the pain. If you're serious about building a platform of financially fluency—you'll rearrange other priorities to make time.

- Drip, drip, drip. This approach was suggested when we were talking about how to fit financial education into the lives of busy parents. It is no less relevant here. At Sam's Council meetings, family members took thirty minutes to skim newspapers and magazines, and each member of the family circled three headlines they had questions about or thought might have relevance to family assets. Then they discussed what impact those headlines would have on their investments in the near term as well as the long term. Sam took one or more of his kids to company briefings, and they each practiced the creation of a mixed portfolio and presented their thinking to one another. Though they had a financial educator who helped guide the process, it was the combined experiences that, over time (drip, drip, drip), had the effect of building financial consciousness in each of his adult children.

- Coinvesting. Modeling correct or good behavior is not just for teaching our kids to wipe their feet when they come in from outside or helping them learn how to change a tire; it is relevant for investing as well. Offering to seed or match a small portfolio or new investment gives you the opportunity to teach children about the tools and process of investing, as well as giving them "skin in the game"—both yours and theirs—to make it a real and possibly lucrative lesson. You'll be surprised how well this works, too.

- Competition. Just as nurturing gives young people confidence to learn investing without fear, so can a little rivalry ignite their competitive spirit. Consider challenging the young adult to see who can make the wisest investments over a period of nine months. Or make the stakes lower by setting a rate of return to beat over the course of a year. Just make sure you temper the competitive spirit with sound judgment and limits. Aggressive investing or day trading, like gambling, can become a compulsive or addictive habit if not managed properly.

INVESTING IN THE NEXT GENERATION

A contemporary temptation is to invest in an adult child's business idea. *They might learn something*, you rationalize. *Maybe they'll be the next Zuckerberg*, you hope. But unless you're clear about the difference between investment and subsidy, this strategy is fraught with pitfalls. A subsidy is fundamentally a gift. You don't expect a return (unless it is explicitly structured as a loan), except in ways you will both be proud of: eventual self-reliance, mastery of new skills, and independence. However, a responsible investment—philanthropic or commercial—demands a planned return. To pretend that money given for an idea is an investment, when it's really a way to give them money in a manner that preserves a little dignity, is just wrong. If you want kids to learn about investing, invest—preparing for both risk and reward.

Young adults who show an interest in making a job, not just taking a job, are already ahead of the game, and you want to encourage this impulse toward twenty-first-century self-employment. But keep it real. Whether you're investing $100 in the purchase of a domain name for their new website or $100,000 in seed funding for a new technology, the rules are the same: serious planning, due diligence, risk management, and transparency with both finances and expectations.

But what if a large investment in entrepreneurial experience is feasible and seems like a good thing to do for a highly motivated kid? Let's assume that your amazing twenty-something has a good idea, lots of energy, and great passion (and sees a way to participate in one of the great disruptive developments of the twenty-first century!)—maybe even some relevant experience and partners who complement his skill set. He pitches the idea. How do you respond? We know families for whom the investment in a child (or in-law) has been a great experience. The kid makes money; the family realizes a return; and pride reigns throughout. The next generation is focused on wealth building, not just living on legacy. How great is that?

The Family Investment Fund. How the "investment" in the first lemonade stand was handled is a clue to how families will handle investments in adult children. If you practiced radical honesty when they were seven, the practice will seem like normal family policy today. But if you bought all the ingredients for the lemonade, then purchased the finished product so the kids would "make" some money, you will need to set new ground rules for this adult venture, being very clear about your own capacity to lose money. If you can't afford to lose it, don't offer it up. And even *if* you can afford to lose the money you invest, keep these guidelines in mind:

- **Demand seriousness.** Treat them as the adults they are and as business partners, giving them the respect and obligations that accompany it. Ask hard questions and insist on a serious, rigorous business plan. Give them the help they need to create a solid plan if necessary, but making an investment based on hopes and promises does no favor to the would-be entrepreneur. It's a setup for future failure.
- **Make it real.** If you loan or invest, make sure you have documents to track and explain the transaction. This is how that twenty-two-year-old rookie becomes a financially mature businessperson. And don't hide "incidental" costs such as office supplies or attorney's fees. Just as with

dieting or managing cash outflow, *all* costs are significant and real, and they should be transparent. If your kid grabs a notebook and pen from the desk in the den in order to show you the next great mousetrap, account for those supplies as a business expense—after all, someone had to buy them in the first place.

- **Due diligence.** It's self-evident that making an investment in an adult child, no matter how accomplished he or she is, without doing due diligence is a bad model to set. Ask for a business plan, and then do your own due diligence. If they actually are going to run a business, start a nonprofit, or write the next great American novel, they will need to have a plan to sustain their vision. Doing your due diligence is the act of a good mentor—and may turn up information that could help their business success. Do it, and don't write any checks until the process is complete.

- **Establish family policies.** What cap will you put on your investment? What are your minimum requirements for investment? What milestones must be met? If you have other children, answering these questions is imperative. What practices have worked in the past and what precedent might this set? Exceptions are fine, but when family policies are clear and explicit, next-generation entrepreneurs can be prepared for what they have to do to get a family investment.

- **Avoid crisis investment.** Businesses fail because of competition that is too good to overcome, undercapitalization that is realized too late to correct, bad assumptions, and poor execution. Earlier I recommended that when a child makes a mistake with her allowance the question is not, "What did you do wrong?" but "What did you learn?" The same is true for the failed enterprise. If the business or nonprofit really cannot or should not be salvaged, the best course is to allow the learning to begin. However much you want to protect your children from the harshness of business, early failure is almost inevitable and offsetting the pain is a bounty of learning opportunities. Often the imperatives of due diligence, healthy balance sheets, and financial sustainability come in the second business, not the first. Don't rob them of teachable moments by protecting them as though they are still children. Do encourage them to pick themselves up and try again.

Of course, these are all actions you would take for any investment you are considering. Many investors say they invest in people, not ideas. If your kids are not yet those people, help them become the person you will invest in. Say, "Let me help you get ready," not just "No" or, worse, "Yes" with misgivings.

3. Entrepreneurs: Embracing Their Weirdness

Plenty of young people are making contributions to medicine, law, science, engineering, and a host of other disciplines by gaining advanced degrees and joining companies as they have been doing for centuries. We still need disciplined organizations to manage large-scale enterprises. But the "company woman" has been joined by the rise of a new entrepreneurial class: young people with the means and knowledge to manipulate twenty-first-century tools for their own independent ventures and awareness of fields that were once the stuff of sci-fi writers. Given young people's abilities to reach vast audiences with a short clip on YouTube or create an animated story with inexpensive software that was once the province of only the most well-resourced companies, families may find they are living with a whole new species of offspring.

Whether it's the nineteen-year-old with a plan to save the world by raising money and traveling to Rwanda to run a project for Kiva, or the twenty-five-year-old who, inspired to create an entertainment pod in space, raises money on Kickstarter.com to fund initial research, it's clear we have a new generation that can and will shun the organization for a blank canvas of their own. These are young people for whom the structures of the organization are less alluring than the opportunity to express their own visions—to embrace their "weirdness" in an effort to make something new and different.

Parenting this new breed of independent "imagineers" can be a harrowing task. In the last decade, two movies took off that celebrated the pain and possibilities of individualism: in 2008 the documentary *Man on Wire* unpacked the life and times of Philippe Petit, famous for his 1974 tightrope walk between the twin towers of the World Trade Center. Petit may strike some as the epitome of individual weirdness, but his passion and commitment to living his own story are as inspiring and exhilarating as his famous walk. And the 2010 film *The Social Network* chronicles the early days of Facebook and the trials and tribulations that Mark Zuckerberg faced as a "weird genius," both positively and negatively. If you saw either of those films, you can imagine what it might be like to find yourself living with Petit or Zuckerberg—how do you mentor the adult child whose vision is so far beyond your own experience that you seem to be talking across the stars, from one planet to another? How do you know whether, as a parent, you are giving wise counsel or irrelevant advice from another age? How can you tell whether that young adult you raised is talking nonsense or on the brink of a breakthrough invention?

This is one of the great challenges of twenty-first-century parenting. When asked about the parenting of Mark Zuckerberg in the February 4, 2011, edition of the *Salt Lake Tribune*, the Facebook founder's father said he and his wife felt their job was to support their children's strengths and passions with a balance of work and play. "Probably the best thing I can say is something that my wife and I have always believed in," he said. "Rather than impose upon your kids or try and steer their lives in a certain direction, to recognize what their strengths are and support their strengths and support the development of the things they're passionate about."

Grounded and commonsensical—once again we return to the value of financial fundamentals. No matter how cutting-edge the idea or how sci-fi-amazing the venture, your offspring needs to understand that even if you can build a business plan with no profit for ten years, you will eventually need to find a way to sustain yourself—and the idea. You must be sufficiently financially fluent to create a narrative that supports your vision, complete with the operational specificity that will encourage others to trust enough to invest in and support whatever weirdness is on the table.

There is an enduring need for the universal tools with which to make a case for one's vision. "I need money because it's a really good idea" has to morph into "I need $X that will result in X result in X time and can provide X return on the investment (social and/or financial)."

Many next-generation members feel strongly that they are safer and more secure creating their own jobs rather than depending on the uncertainties of economic storms and other people's decisions. The courage it takes to think of entrepreneurship as self-defense is not insignificant, but if you are raising next-generation entrepreneurs, you are raising leaders who will be regenerators of a new and healthy economy.

Moving On

Whether adult children are simply late bloomers with the energy and passions of the newly awake, or they slept through their financial apprenticeship and are still loathe to wake up, your job is to be constant in your vision for a financially fluent family. It is hard work, requiring stamina, intention, and modeling.

But I've had the good fortune to see, over and over, the human return on investment for families who have in fact made the effort: it infuses them with family cohesion, shared vision, and a spirit of cooperation. It creates a learning culture, a culture in which families share the joy of learning together, not just the tedium of accounting for one's financial accounts. And the payoff for the next generation ripples out in values that reflect the best values of the nation: leadership, sustainability, contribution, and invention.

After every talk I give, invariably there are at least a few people who approach me with a story I have now heard literally hundreds of times. It always begins with "My mother always said; my father always told me. . . ." Over time, it finally hit me: those grown-ups were reporting what their parents (or grand-parents) had nagged them about as children. Those "naggings" had, over time, morphed into core values, character.

So now I remind the families I work with that Marketing 101 is just nagging made professional (repeat, repeat, repeat)—and that conscientious parents should nag to their heart's content, secure in the knowledge that values, repeated and reinforced often enough, become the character of the next generation.

Side Trips

"Service is the rent
we pay for living."

MARIAN WRIGHT EDELMAN,
FOUNDER AND PRESIDENT OF THE CHILDREN'S DEFENSE FUND

Raising Young Philanthropists

Thomas Jefferson said: "I deem it the duty of every man to devote a certain portion of his income for charitable purposes and that it is his further duty to see it so applied as to do the most good of which it is capable. This I believe to be best insured by keeping within the circle of his own inquiry and information the subjects of distress to whose relief his contributions shall be applied."

David Ben-Gurion, the first prime minister of Israel, said: "The activities of the state of Israel will not be guided solely by economic and political considerations. We would be untrue to ourselves if we ignore the great moral inheritance of our prophets and sages. In that inheritance we inherit the social and humane visions of brotherhood, social justice, and freedom. The state of Israel will be judged, ultimately by the loyalty to the sublime dictate of Judaism: 'Thou shalt love thy neighbor as thyself.'"

Both men, historically over a century apart, were acknowledging that what makes countries (and communities) work are the mitigating factors of reciprocity, caring, and concern for the whole community, not just portions of it. Capital markets and political considerations alone will not serve the population's needs for security and well-being.

According to VolunteeringInAmerica.gov, an estimated 62.8 million American adults formally volunteered roughly 8.1 billion hours in 2011.

What are your children prepared to give?

Families are loath to speak to outsiders about their own children's shortcomings. But I am struck by how often mothers, grandparents, aunts, godparents, and close family friends approach me and, in quiet whispers, describe a child who they feel is excessively self-absorbed, disconnected from the needs of others, and seemingly obsessed by the popular culture and the things the culture hawks as desirable. With despair, as though it is a futile quest, they ask whether there is anything they can do that will result in a less mall-focused kid. Philanthropic activity is one path that can help kids see beyond "stuff."

Encouraging the Generous Impulse

Philanthropy is as individual as a thumbprint, and exposing young people to the variety of ways in which they can be engaged in philanthropy (over and above simply giving money away) is a way of showing them a larger world, offering them an expanded menu of options with which they can explore the world and their place in it. Here are a few of the items on that menu.

Volunteerism: Kids can volunteer in schools, hospitals, museums, shelters. They can run for a cause or clean up a hiking trail with friends; they can help out at a food bank (and not just on Thanksgiving) or deliver groceries to the next-door neighbor. They can walk dogs at the humane society or raise money for that family whose house burned last month. Even very young children can participate in the act of volunteerism.

Philanthropy: Kids can practice philanthropy by giving money, goods, or services. We encourage a philanthropic allocation in the allowance to inculcate the value of contributing to the needs of others. Taxes support the vital workings of the community, large and small: the physical infrastructure, safety, and so on. But in our current era of fractured civil discourse, private citizens are called on to support a wide variety of needs. This means young people have an opportunity to choose ways and places to give that reflect who they are: gifts to the Children's Museum for sponsored admissions for children who cannot afford to visit and financial contributions to that food bank they give time to are just two of an endless range of possibilities for gifts to give back. Children are often pretty headline-savvy; they will have ideas about where they want their money to go. Particularly in the beginning, allow them to follow their interests; over time they will develop discriminating judgment.

Social enterprise: Exposing young people to businesses and nonprofits whose missions serve a dual purpose of making money and making a difference (self-sustaining contributions, as it were) is an opportunity to introduce the topic of economics. Regardless of your own leanings, this hybrid business concept is a great way to explore complex business ideas. When buying yogurt, you can discuss why you might choose Stonybrook over Yoplait or Timberland shirts over Gap.

Faith-based social services: From the saintly good works of Mother Teresa to the social services of the Salvation Army, and especially if your family is committed to the work of your faith, you can engage children in tithing and missions very early on.

Social activism and advocacy: High school and college students often make up the ranks of the underpaid, underappreciated few who work to mitigate the

A Glossary of Philanthropy

Send your kids in search of the meanings for the following terms (feel free to add your own to this list). Offer cash to the charity of their choice for each term learned.

Charity

Grassroots

Development

Philanthropy

Challenge grant

Discretionary funds

Donor

Donee

Endowment

Grant

Pledge

Site visit

RFP

Social entrepreneur

Trust/Trustee

harm of the many. If your teen or college student expresses an interest in working for a group such as the Innocence Project (rights of prisoners) or water.org (clean water access), this may open doors to a career or education focus while they explore the economics and politics of making a difference.

Research: Service can be expressed in many ways, and the child who wants to intern at the zoo's animal clinic or the historical society's library has an opportunity to learn with a specific purpose aimed at advocacy, change, education, and advances in the quality of life.

Of course, telling children they need to relinquish a part of their allowance to give away to someone else may not be as instantly satisfying as you think it ought to be. As with so many things that are really good for kids, the joy you express in seeing the impact of your own philanthropic work (as opposed to complaints about all the times you are pressed to give) will model a reality that they will be more likely to aspire to in their own lives.

By making sure kids are philanthropically oriented, you give them vehicles for achieving connectedness with their community—local and global.

Whether your approach to philanthropy is religious, philosophical, or purely pragmatic, by making sure kids are philanthropically oriented you give them vehicles for achieving connectedness with their community—local and global. Nurturing a philanthropic spirit can start very early. When children put quarters in Salvation Army kettles at Christmas, accompany you to drop off canned goods at the homeless shelter, and set aside part of their allowance, they build a consciousness of sharing that will last well beyond the financial apprenticeship.

In chapter 2, I described the concept of a Charity Café night as a peer activity offering an alternative to hanging out at the mall and spending money (see page 32 for instructions for establishing a Charity Café). But kids who get hooked on the excitement of raising and giving away money may find the process is more complex than they anticipated. It's one thing to drop clothes off at Goodwill and call it a tax deduction, quite another to connect one's life passion with a mission to make a difference or even to pragmatically assess who will use donated money in the most effective ways.

The following chart offers a structure for helping kids connect the issues they care about with making a real difference. After listing the issues or causes that matter most to them (this can be done with young people nine and older), they will see what their instincts for allocating money to these causes tell them about their own priorities. See the following page for specific instructions.

Category	Organization	Amount of Time	Amount of Money	Heart Score
Health				
Animal Issues				
Environment				
Social Justice/ Human Rights				
Arts and Education				
Sports				
Other				

a. For each category, fill in the name(s) of one or more organizations offering opportunities for change or involvement.

b. Using six hours each week to donate to one or more of the organizations listed, allocate your time.

c. Using $10,000 to give away over a twelve-month period to one or more of the organizations you listed, allocate your money.

d. On a scale of 1 to 10, 1 equaling a cold heart and 10 equaling a heart full of care, rate the concern you have for each of the organizations or issues you have listed.

e. Now take a close look at the chart: are the heart score, the way money was allocated, and the way time was allocated all in sync?

Once a clear picture of what matters to your children begins to emerge, encourage them to look into a range of local programs that match their interests—call or write for materials on each organization, and as their interest grows, visit the programs.

Philanthropy provides a tool for galvanizing kids to master the other nine basic money skills; it also offers an antidote to a mass culture that places far too much value on consuming and accumulating things and money for image and status. Encouraging philanthropic engagement early plays a critical role in helping kids develop a sense of purpose and meaning. Kids who feel they are part of something greater than themselves become more grounded, self-confident adults. Wherever kids' passions happen to lie, feeling a moral imperative that connects their own interests and privileges to the needs of others will give them a greater sense of community and connectedness in their lives.

Philanthropy Resources

The Art of Giving: Where the Soul Meets a Business Plan,
Charles Bronfman and Jeffrey Solomon

Getting to Giving: Fundraising the Entrepreneurial Way, Howard H. Stevenson

Give Smart: Philanthropy That Gets Results, Thomas Tierney and Joe Fleishman

The Giving Family: Raising Our Children to Help Others, Susan Crites Price
(available through the Council on Foundations, www.cof.org)

Inspired Philanthropy: Your Step-by-Step Guide to Creating a Giving Plan,
Tracy Gary and Melissa Kohner

Volunteer Vacations: Short-Term Vacations That Will Benefit You and Others,
Bill McMillon

The Measure of Our Success: A Letter to My Children and Yours,
Marian Wright Edelman

Online resource for family volunteering projects: www.familycares.org

Kids Care Clubs: www.kidscare.org

The Foundation Center: www.fdncenter.org

The Virtual Foundation: www.virtualfoundation.org

Network for Good: www.networkforgood.org

Youth NOISE: www.youthnoise.com

"In a country well governed,
poverty is something
to be ashamed of.
In a country badly governed,
wealth is something
to be ashamed of."

—CONFUCIUS

It's Not Just About the Kids

I t's not just about the money, I said at the beginning of the book, and as I close, this time around, I feel compelled to say, it's not just about the kids—it's also about the context that we, as grown-ups, create for them. Just as we have an obligation to create a safe and loving home environment in which they can learn to be financially fit, we have a responsibility to create communities that are safe and rich with opportunity. And we have a duty to steward our national assets—human and financial in the mode of one nation.

But as I write, I fear we've created a deeply polarized nation. In the 1980s, I worked at the Polaroid corporation and understood polarization as a scientific property that gave us sunglasses able to cut through glare—a good thing that literally allowed us to *see* better. But the polarization that wracks our country today is a bad thing because it distorts vision. We *see* through the tint of ideology and do not rise to the level of thoughtful consideration that is needed to tackle some of our long-term problems.

The notion of one nation is more a blur than a clear vision. How, then, can we create a national environment that is a healthy environment in which to raise kids? How can we transcend this polarization to embrace differences while strengthening the one nation we inhabit together? We begin at home. We model the ability to transcend deep polarization with the faith that, years from now, children who have seen something other than rancorous sniping across the news cycles will know there is another way to run a family, grow a community, and lead a country. They will have seen how to avoid the temptation to polarize; they will have skills to find ways forward that are more effective than a simplistic us versus them.

So how can we model for children the ability to transcend polarization? My personal "Aha!" moment on this came with a picture on the front page of the *New York Times.*

It is the nature of my work that I engage with families at all points on the political spectrum. Conservatives and liberals agree on one thing: a financially fluent child is a secure child, with the tools and knowledge to make sound economic choices, whatever those may be. So when the Occupy movement first emerged, I made a quiet decision not to engage my clients, many of whom are comfortably part of the "1 percent," in discussions about their personal views on the demonstrations that were then dominating headlines. I'm an educator, not a politician, and I try to model staying open to learning, finding ways to communicate across great differences. Tapping into what was then a highly polarizing topic was not going to be fruitful, I thought.

Then one day a picture appeared on the front page of the *New York Times* of young Occupy Movement demonstrators holding a sign that read: *"We're part of the 1 percent, and we don't approve!"* My first thought was: Yikes, conversation at Thanksgiving is going to be difficult now!

At that point I realized that backing away from hard conversations, polarizing conversations, is not the answer. Avoidance is not an effective strategy. Allowing families to be torn apart because they don't have tools to bridge a divide of values and priorities is as wrong as tearing the country apart because we can no longer talk, compromise, and share a common vision for "one nation." I had an obligation to provide better solutions to my clients. I had to dive in.

And so, as we come to the end of this edition of *Raising Financially Fit Kids*, I'm adding an eleventh skill: *transcending polarization*. This skill does not require advanced education in economics or political theory beyond an understanding that, regardless of political affiliation or ideology, civic duty is required of us all. A free economy—the kind that has enabled family businesses like the one I grew up in or small companies like the one I own—is kept healthy and productive when citizens balance the good of their community, state, and nation with personal beliefs and goals. Family life and citizenship depend on sharing a vision, listening to one another, and developing a habit of tolerance.

Throughout the book I encourage parents to set boundaries, be consistent, and function as the grown-up, leader, and sage. However, we must put this in the context of understanding that the world is not ours—it always belongs to the next generation. There comes a moment—sometimes when they're fourteen, sometimes when they're twenty-four—when you have to acknowledge the wisdom and courage your children bring to their own lives. In truth, this is what you're preparing them for. The family picture may not be developing as you had originally dreamed it—but it may be a better picture in the long run.

For the sake of the children growing up in your homes—and our health as a nation—we must develop the skill, and the will, to transcend polarization. Throughout the book, I've used scenarios to demonstrate how to imbue children with financial skills at different points in the developmental process. To offer some guidance for honing the ability to transcend polarization within the family, I offer the following examples.

The Economic Divide

We return to that photo in the *New York Times* to demonstrate how a family might respond to the situation. One can imagine the phone call that went from one generation to the next as soon as the picture was published:

Dad (to his daughter, who was holding the sign): WHAT ARE YOU THINKING? Do you realize how embarrassing this is for me?

Daughter: That's the point, Dad. You should be embarrassed. Our lifestyle and the way you finance it are shameful.

Dad: Our money allows you to attend the school you chose; it paid for your trip to India; and it pays for the hybrid that you drove to the demonstration— it's hypocritical to take my money and then demonstrate publicly against it. Perhaps you'd feel closer to your cause if I took you out of the will.

Daughter: Fine, if that's how you feel, you can disinherit me. But I'd rather fight for a cause I believe in than be part of the problem.

This conversation rapidly degenerates into stark judgments about one another's values and economic choices. In a short and powerful exchange, father and daughter are both likely to stake out sides from which they may find themselves looking at one another across a divide too wide to bridge.

How might this dad have transcended polarization? Imagine an alternative conversation:

Dad (to his daughter, who was holding the sign): You're embarrassing me in front of my colleagues, but I have to admit, I'm proud you're standing up for what you believe in. I just wish you hadn't made it so public.

Daughter: I didn't mean to embarrass you, Dad, but I've been saying these things for years, and you don't listen to me. This movement is important to me. My generation is inheriting a lot of economic and social problems, and it's up to us to fix them.

Dad: Fair enough, but just as you're troubled by the way I live my values and choices, the way you're living your values and choices right now is putting stress on me—and your family. I'll commit to staying open to your point of view, and of course I can't stop you from exercising your rights, but I ask that we both get more informed. I'd like you to meet some of my friends who are running businesses that employ a lot of people—they have a perspective on this too—and I'd like to spend time talking with your friends. I'll read some of your favorite writings on this subject if you'll read some of mine. Let's keep talking, Susan; we're one family, and we need to find a way to understand one another

Daughter: Okay, Dad, but this has to be real or it won't work.

Dad: I know. We can ask your mom to keep us both real!

Roll your eyes if you must, but when generations commit to learning *from one another*—and follow through on a plan—the family as a whole and each of its members benefit. The day of the all-knowing patriarch is long gone (if it ever existed). Civil discourse must be modeled in families if it is going be alive in the larger spheres of business and governance.

Lifestyle Divide

The principle is always the same: reframe the conversation from oppositional positions to a common goal. In this case, Tim has decided to drop out of college to pursue what he describes as a lifelong interest in climbing mountains, leading hikes in distant locales, and teaching others to enjoy the great outdoors. His parents have been saving for his college education since he was born. As he turns twenty-one, can these two world views mesh? Will not living up to his parents' expectations derail the family relationship?

Tim: I know you're disappointed that I don't want to finish college, but I'm in top physical condition for climbing now, and if I don't take advantage of the shape I'm in, who knows if I can do it later?

Parents: Fine, but don't expect us to pay for your adventure. We were making an investment in your future. We're not paying for an extended vacation.

Tim: Why isn't this a good investment? As a top flight climber, I can lead *National Geographic* hikes, I can participate in rescue missions. It's a different education, but it's an education.

Parents: And what are you gong to do when you're fifty? What happens if you suffer a major injury? A good education is the safety net we are giving you. If you don't finish college, we're going to cut you off.

Tim: Okay, fine. I'm lining up sponsors to underwrite my climbs. I don't need your money. And don't expect to see me home anytime soon.

Again, opposing positions that lead to a fracture in the family. Imagine this replay:

Tim: I'm leaving school in December to join the Swiss climbing team. I know you want me to graduate from college, but I'm in peak physical condition now, and I want to explore a different kind of education.

Parents: What we want is for you to lead a satisfying, meaningful life. Our vision includes a college education to do that, but if you're prepared for the challenges that dropping out now may cause down the road, we'll support you. While you're getting started we'll contribute 50 percent of what we would have paid for college to your mountain fund—through the time you would have graduated. But you have to come home at least twice a year so we can catch up and see how you're doing.

Tim: Why don't you join me for part of one of my hikes? I know you two hiked before you had us kids—why not start again?

This is not rocket science. From oppositional positions that leave no room for common ground to a shared family vision is not such a long distance. It does require imagination and a willingness to see more than one solution to a family challenge. It also calls for a willingness to learn from children. There's a reason companies recruit the young: they want the fresh, innovative ideas that come with the perspective of youth. That fresh POV can be an asset for families as well.

I grew up in Maine, and two things fueled an appreciation for the skill of transcending polarization in the family and in the nation. One influence was Margaret Chase Smith, the Republican senator from Maine. She was a beacon of civility and moderation, and—though she would likely not have been pleased to know it—a feminist role model: my first experience of a powerful, independent woman. It was the complexity of her life and politics that helped me understand that as humans, we are rarely as simplistic as a single party, a single position—we are a complicated mix of views, positions, and experiences. It is that complexity that makes us rich, contributing members of a family and a society.

The other influence was the town meetings of my childhood. Perhaps only the Iowa caucuses are closer to pure democracy than a New England town meeting. And though they can be *very* exciting, they can also be raucous, unruly, divisive exercises in posturing and self-interest. Though the founding fathers seem to have practiced pure democracy in their inner circles (small groups, lots of discussion, a long-term view of how to work together), there was a reason they designed representative democracy into the workings of the federal government. They understood that "my way or the highway" could cause a country—or indeed a family—to break apart. Their original design forced imaginative dialogue, innovative solutions, shared visions.

Whether you vote Republican and your kids vote Democratic or the other way around; whether you give to Israel and they give to the Palestinians; and whether you eat vegan and they eat carnivorously is less important than that you find a way to be in conversation. It is in the family that we raise thoughtful, contributing members of community. It is in the family that we have a chance to raise financially fit kids—citizens of one great nation.

"You are the teacher and the taught and the teaching."

—KRISHNAMURTI

Frequently Asked Questions

In case of emergency, you can turn to this last chapter for brief answers to the top questions I am most frequently asked.

Q. How much should we give our kids for an allowance?

A. It varies. Remember, an allowance is a tool for practicing money skills; it is not a salary (for chores), an entitlement (just because you can), or for behavior modification (*If you don't behave . . .*). The allowance should reflect real ways to manage money—whether just having three jars (giving, saving, spending) to manage when they are six; or managing after-school activities when they are twelve or thirteen. See page 51 for more on this topic.

Q. I probably know less about my finances than my kids know. How can I help them when I am such a beginner myself?

A. Historically no one had anything resembling the kind of financial education I advocate in this book. Prior to the 1980s, the financial world was more regulated and less complex. Prior to the 1980s—and the ease of e-trade that Charles Schwab introduced—only a very small group of people *could* be very involved in complex finance. Today, financial education is economic self-defense, and everyone needs it. Whether you are six or sixty, mastery of the Ten Basic Money Skills is relevant. Don't worry about being an expert for your kids; use this opportunity to learn with them.

Q. When should we tell our kids about [trust funds, family assets, family debts, and so on]?

A. When they are ready. There is no magic age at which financial transparency is appropriate. Some thirteen-year-olds are ready for disclosures that some eighteen-year-olds cannot yet handle. Transparency should follow readiness, and readiness comes from mastering the Ten Basic Money Skills.

Q. My children's friends' families do not have the same level of assets we do—how do we help them not feel awkward?

A. Wealth is not just about the money; it is about the human capital each of us is equipped with. If you are emphasizing the value of human capital in your own family, your children will recognize and value it in their friends. See page 15 for instructions on how to create a True Wealth Audit.

Q. We're part of the 99 percent, not part of the 1 percent, and we struggle to make ends meet. We can't afford to give our kids an allowance—how then can we teach our kids money skills?

A. Chances are you are giving your kids an invisible allowance already—if you are keeping them in shelter and food, you are providing an "allowance." And in this case the task of developing mastery is almost easier. Share the utility bill with them and ask for suggestions for how to reduce it next month. Share the monthly food budget and challenge them to help build family menus that produce great meals and lower food bills.

Q. My son just maxed out his credit card for the third time. I don't want his credit rating to be affected, but I can't afford to keep bailing him out. What do I do?

A. Stop. Although it may be painful to watch kids get into trouble, sometimes big mistakes are their greatest teachers. One alternative is to pay off the card and write a new contract with your son to pay you back, with the agreement that not honoring the contract will result in the loss of some privilege (does he have access to the family car? Is he using your vacation house?). Behavior has consequences, and eventually you will have the opportunity to help him experience that. Don't stand in the way of a teachable moment!

Q. I think entrepreneurs are born, not made. What's the point of teaching entrepreneurship? My kids are going to study the arts anyway.

A. The jury is still out on the nature/nurture question of entrepreneurship. What is clear is that whether the next gen decides to write a novel, practice medicine, act on stage, be a rock star, or head for the major leagues, they will each need the skills to create and manage their own financial safety net. As we think about entrepreneurship, we do not assume every kid is going to start a business in the conventional sense—but they will need to know how to manage cash flow, understand a balance sheet, and safeguard their credit ratings. Those are basic entrepreneurial skills.

Q. I think philanthropy is important, but my kids seem unable to identify anything they care enough about to give to. How can I get them excited about making a difference?

A. Childhood is a notoriously self-absorbed time of life. Don't fight the resistance; go with their real interests. Which volunteer activities will open doors for them? Are they interested in going to the Berklee School of Music? Involvement in a charity that gives instruments to kids would look good on their college application. Do they aspire to be a major league coach? Supporting youth sports and Special Olympics can't hurt. If they only collect superhero comic books, insisting that they donate a comic book to a homeless shelter for each one they buy for themselves will at least remind them there are kids in homeless shelters. Co-opt your kids' interests to help them make a difference for others.

Q. But my kid is twenty-four and still has no interests. Now what?

A. This is typically just a reflection of a young adult's undeveloped identity or sense of self. Often these are late bloomers, and they require one of two things: exposure to a wide variety of people and experiences and/or clear expectations ("In this family it's important to give back—if you do not have a goal or interest to focus your philanthropic responsibility this year, I'll give a gift in your name to something I care about for your birthday.").

Q: How do we help our daughter become financially independent?

A. When it comes to money, gender matters. There is an ingrained assumption (though it is finally fading) that little boys will be breadwinners and little girls will have the choice of breadwinners. The numbers bear out the sad consequences of this assumption. Parents who want to have independent daughters must do three things to battle this.

First, Daddy's little girl can do math. Letting girls off the hook when it comes to financial accountability sabotages her long-term success. No matter how adorable she is, make sure your Princess knows you expect her to save money, not just spend it.

Second, the next time your daughter comes to you with an idea for a business or a question about money—no matter how naïve the query—resist any urge to call her behavior or plans "cute." Remember that she is practicing the concepts and language of money that will help her become self-confident and self-reliant.

Third, immerse her in a sea of positive role models. She may not want to hear you lecture her on why she needs to be financially prepared (the future can seem far away to an adolescent or teen), but she may listen to stories from other women. Assemble an all-women money mentor team and line them up for a month of after school events or Saturday morning visits. Give her well-written woman-oriented books for birthdays, good grades, or no reason at all. This chorus of voices will give her permission to explore and make mistakes, to see herself as having something in common with these clearly interesting, financially independent women.

Q. But what about boys. Aren't they at risk too?

A. Absolutely. The cause and effect are fundamentally different, but boys are significantly impacted by assumptions around gender and money. We expect a lot from our young men. We expect them to earn the money, to pay for their dates, and to know about money. This empowers many, but it cripples others. Because boys are expected to know things, they are frequently ashamed when they do not. Our old joke about men being afraid to ask for directions can have calamitous consequences when it comes to finance and debt. Volunteer your knowledge and wisdom to the boys in your life; give them practice in financial decision making and problem solving.

Q. What can I do to help my son?

A. Just as with girls, check your assumptions. Know that no one is born knowing this stuff, and reassure your son of the same. We need to be taught. We need to make mistakes. We need practice. This is how boys become men. Understand that boys feel societal pressure to earn big and spend big. Years after they've left the playground, they may still feel that the boy with the most toys wins. To help your son avoid the morass of debt and materialism, help him claim a sense of who he is apart from the benchmarks for success that he thinks he's supposed to exhibit. Encourage his passions. Remind him that his self-worth is not his net worth. And, most important, model this behavior yourself.

And follow the suggestions for girls, applied to boys with an all-male team. (Some would call this the old boys' network that has always been in place—but the old boys tend to take care of one another, which is not the same as teaching and empowering one another.)

About the Author

© Cindy Pitou Burton

Since 1992, JOLINE GODFREY has been a pioneer in the movement to increase financial intelligence among young people and families. She is the CEO of Independent Means, Inc., and an advisor to families around the world. Previous books include *Our Wildest Dreams: Women Making Money, Having Fun, Doing Good*; *No More Frogs to Kiss: 99 Ways to Give Economic Power to Girls*; and *Twenty $ecrets to Money and Independence: The DollarDiva's Guide to Life*. A former Kellogg Fellow, she holds degrees from the University of Maine and an M.S.W. from Boston University and was awarded an honorary degree in business from Bentley College. She lives in Ojai, California.

Index